HOW TO DEVELOP
YOUR PERSONALITY

Metropolitan Youssef

ST MARY & MOSES
ABBEY PRESS

How to Develop Your Personality
By Metropolitan Youssef

Designed & Published by:
St. Mary & St. Moses Abbey Press
101 S Vista Dr, Sandia, TX 78383
stmabbeypress.com

Translation from Arabic by St. Mary & St. Moses Abbey.

Contents

Introduction

Some of [our] children may face various problems and hardships, predisposing them in the future to crises; [these crises] result from their exposure to mistakes which had taken place during the stages of their upbringing. Some of these mistakes may be unintentional, and consequently, we need to understand how the human being grows and [what are] the stages of development of his personality, and what are the factors that influence his growth, till we reach the goal for the sake of which God created man; namely, that we may be conformed to the image of Christ: "For whom He foreknew, He also predestined to be conformed to the image of His Son."[1] Also, that he may grow himself from glory to glory till he comprehends this goal.

The same is also said by Paul the Apostle in his epistle to the Colossians, "Him we preach, warning every man and teaching every man in all wisdom,

---

1   Romans 8:29.

that we may present every man perfect in Christ Jesus."[2]

This matter is not far from every person, though his family may have made mistakes in his upbringing. For he is able, by the grace of God and His work in his life, to change himself and develop his personality till he reaches the image of Christ.

Unfortunately, when a person speaks about his problems which are the result of erroneous upbringing, he does not find truthful advice from others—perhaps due to their lack of knowledge— but what these [people] say may trouble him all the more. This is [exactly] what happened with Job when his friends came to give him comfort. He said to them, "Miserable comforters are you all!"[3]

Therefore, the afflicted person who is suffering because of mistakes in his upbringing, needs sympathy and understanding of his condition, more than anything else. As the Scripture says in the Book of Job, "To him who is afflicted, kindness should be shown by his friend, even though he forsakes the fear of the Almighty."[4] This means that the afflicted person, whose affliction and sorrows are caused by others, needs kindness and sympathy, even though the fear of God is not in his heart. Because if we show him love, kindness, and sympathy, the fear of

---

2   Colossians 1:28.

3   Job 16:2.

4   Job 6:14.

the Almighty may return to him.

Therefore, for a person to obtain healing from any [sort of] suffering, he needs to understand how to grow and develop himself. Likewise, these around him need to understand, themselves too, what the factors of growth are. Perhaps, for example, there is a person suffering from depression, or from a feeling of guilt, because of the mistakes [done] in his upbringing when he was young. For this, in essence, may be due to that these essential factors for growth were not observed, in spite of their importance for the healing of the soul and sound growth. This is what Paul the Apostle meant when he said, "Be transformed by the renewing of your mind."[5] This means that when a person has a new mind-set[6] with which he understands what the factors for sound growth are, he is able to be transformed, and is able to develop himself and his personality, no matter what mistakes had taken place in his upbringing.

Yes, there is hope for healing and change into the image of God.

---

5   Romans 12:2.
6   Or: thought.

1

Factors of Growth

Grace and Truth

We cannot separate grace from truth, because they are bound together; therefore, our discourse about them will be combined. Grace and truth are two essential things which the Lord Christ brought for the redemption of humanity, and for treating the distorted image, distorted by sin. The Holy Scripture says, "For the law was given through Moses, but grace and truth came through Jesus Christ."[7]

The image of man was distorted after the fall, and he lost the image of God and was no longer conformed to His Son. To become once again conformed to the image of His Son, I need grace and truth.

---

7   John 1:17.

It happens, however, in raising our children, or when we deal with the congregation at church, that we separate between grace and truth; so either we deal with grace alone, or we deal with truth alone. If we separate grace from truth, grace is no longer called grace, and likewise, if we separate truth from grace, truth is no longer called truth. Grace and truth have to be bound together. So what do we mean by grace and truth?

Grace is a free gift, given on the basis of the goodness of the giver, and not on the worthiness of the one to whom it is given. When someone is gracious to another, this means that he offers him a free gift, of which the other person is not worthy, because if he were worthy of it, in this case it would be [considered] a reward or a repayment for a good deed he did and is deserving of a reward for it. There is no connection at all between grace and worthiness; it is given only based on the goodness of the giver. And this is what we praise the Lord with, in the Second Canticle, and we say, "O give thanks to the Lord, for He is good: His mercy endures forever." The gift of God is not out of our worthiness, but because He is good and beneficent and His mercy endures forever.

So what is the gift which God has given me? It is His unconditional love. For, had man been worthy of being loved, His love would not have been a gift. But the truth is that I am a sinner; and despite this,

God loves me.

Grace is that God accepts me [while] I am a sinner, as He accepted the adulteress, and as He accepted Zacchaeus the tax collector and the right-hand thief. Grace was made manifest in His acceptance of sinners.

A person has to feel God's love and others' love for him, so that his soul may be healed. This love is not offered him based on his worthiness, but is given to him as grace. Here lies the problem: the servant at church loves the children who are obedient, well-behaved, and "sweet;" does he also love the irritating kid who is a troublemaker? Does he accept him or not? If the servant were dealing [with others] by grace, grace would help this kid change and be reformed, thereby becoming an excellent child in whom is the image of God.

Likewise, parents, too, love their obedient son and daughter, but what is their position towards the son or daughter who stirs problems? Are they able to offer them love and acceptance unconditionally, or not? This is *grace*.

It is impossible for a person to be healed or to change, without feeling the grace of God and His faithfulness in His love for him. For grace gives a sense of safety, which is very important.

Fear often takes hold of us when we are praying, because we believe that God will not answer our prayers, because we feel that we are sinners, so how would God answer us?

We read in the Paradise of the Monks the following words which someone said to the Lord: "Lord, if You were to hear the prayers of the righteous, this would not be [considered] marvelous, but that you hear the prayers of sinners, this is what is marvelous in You, O God!" God accepts me, despite my knowledge that I am a sinner, because he said, "The one who comes to Me I will by no means cast out."[8] This sense of safety is what makes me gain inner healing, and it makes me run to God, and cast my sins before Him, because God will not cast me out.

The sinful woman who went into Simon the Pharisee's house, if she had doubt about the Lord's accepting her, that He would cast her out instead, she would not have gone there, but she was confident that Christ would accept her. This acceptance is what changed her.

Zacchaeus, too, who wanted to see Jesus, did not know the Lord's position towards him. So what happened? The Lord went to him and said to him, "Zacchaeus, make haste and come down, for today I must stay at your house."[9] Undoubtedly, Zacchaeus must have thought to himself, "Is it possible, Lord, that You come into my house, I the sinful tax collector?" This, however, is grace. This love and this acceptance changed Zacchaeus. Therefore, grace

---

8   John 6:37.
9   Luke 19:5.

is very important for the healing of the soul, and for dealing with the other [person] with love and acceptance.

> *"Let your prayer be completely simple. For both the publican and the prodigal son were reconciled to God by a single phrase."*[10]

—St. John Climacus—

We could say that *grace* is the relational dimension of God's dealings with me and for my sake.

God deals with us through two dimensions: the relational dimension and the disciplinary dimension[11]. Grace represents the relational dimension, meaning that God loves me and accepts me, unconditionally.

However, let us imagine that parents deal with their children by grace only. So what will happen? The children will act according to their inclination, and as they wish: they come in and go out as they wish, come home early or late, smoke cigarettes or may take other drugs. Nevertheless, the parents do love them and deal with them with tolerance and acceptance in all matters. A grave problem will result from this, however, represented in that

---

10   Saint John Climacus, *The Ladder of Divine Ascent.* (Boston, MA: Holy Transfiguration Monastery, 2012), 234.

11   Literally: edification-concerned dimension.

these children will practice these behavioral errors repeatedly, till they [i.e. these errors] become inseparable from their personality, because no one is guiding them to what is right and wrong.

Therefore, *truth* has to come along with grace. *Truth* is the disciplinary dimension, and this means the commandment which explains what is right and wrong. I would like to explain something here: When we explain to a person what is right and wrong, this does not make him unworthy, because grace is granted [to the person] regardless of his unworthiness. But God reveals to the person what is right and what is wrong, because He loves him, so He asks the person to stay away from evil, and to commit to doing good. Therefore, truth is the commitment to [following] the commandment; it is the discernment between good and evil. Just as I need an environment in which there is acceptance and grace, for me to grow and change, so, likewise, I need someone to teach me what is right and what is wrong. I need a commandment, which urges me to do this, and not to do that, so that I may turn into[12] the image of God.

If *grace* is the relational dimension of God's dealings with me, then *truth* is the disciplinary dimension of God's dealings with me. It [i.e. truth] constitutes my framework and my conduct, constitutes what I must accept and what I must

---

12   Literally: become in.

reject. If parents were dealing with their children by truth alone—issuing orders, "This is right, and that is wrong," "Do this, and do not do that,"— without offering them any kind of love, acceptance, tolerance, and care, and [if] there were no grace present but only truth, the children would have a void within [them], and a sort of rebellion might arise in them, because the parents' pressure on them is keeping them restrained.

"In the family, the husband and wife have to win each other, thereby they live in peace, do not disagree [with each other] and do not separate [from each other]. Rather, each of them should be considerate of the other's feelings, and each should work at keeping the peace, regardless of how different the perspectives may be on things sometimes. And both should work diligently to always acquire the love of their children, not by way of wrong indulgence, nor by means of harsh strictness, but by caring for them and taking care of them. And so, the family becomes bonded [together]."

—H.H. Pope Shenouda III—

As we have previously said that grace without truth makes the person persist in sin; and truth without grace makes the person rebel, resulting in his failure. There is no one who could keep all the commandments and all the principles, without breaking any of them, and this matter will lead him to the point of despair and rebellion, and anger will be aroused in him.

Rule cares about truth only, and does not care about the human being, as most entities and businesses do. They say, "Business doesn't have heart." What is important to them is the profit the company receives, and the worker who makes a mistake is made to repay. And if the mistake recurred, he would be fired from work. Here they are looking for "right and wrong," without taking into consideration the human being himself.

> *"Winning souls is also necessary in the field of work and management. Everyone who wants a work [to be done], has to gather the workers with him, in a strong bond of devotion to him, and faithfulness in the work. And this [is achieved] by what he shows them, on every occasion, of taking care of them, treating them well, and caring for their material and health needs. So he is not only the boss who gives orders and has the last word, who holds [others] accountable and pronounces punishments, who ensures the soundness of the work with strictness, but he has[13] also a compassionate heart for the workers, is bound to them by*

---

13   Literally: is.

love and loyalty, besides obedience and respect. Winning the souls of the workers and employees is the main assurance for the progress and success of the work, and is an assurance for the work to continue, and to be preserved from demonstrations, strikes, protests, and claims for rights they see unavailable."

—H.H. Pope Shenouda III—

This was the scribes and Pharisees' problem with the Sabbath. They looked for [what is] right and wrong, and did not look for the man, though the commandment was placed for the sake of man. Therefore, the Lord said to them, "The Sabbath was made for man, and not man for the Sabbath."[14] The one who applies the truth, without grace, cares solely about the commandment, [and] not the person. What concerns him is fixing and purging the mistake, without there being mercy or compassion in his approach. Therefore, when they brought the woman caught in the very act, they wanted to stone her. They were not concerned about whether she dies or not, but what concerned them was that this mistake should be purged even if, as a result, this woman was to be stoned. We may have been brought up in homes, or been in a Sunday school [classroom], that favor grace over truth; that is to say, there is in them grace, love and acceptance, without there being any system to specify right

---

14   Mark 2:27.

from wrong. And we may have been brought up in homes or Church, in which there may be nothing but systems, concerned only with right and wrong, without there being [any] sense of the existence of the relational dimension—that is, grace.

This separation between grace and truth is not of the nature of God. This separation, rather, came as a result of sin. Therefore, if you separated grace from truth, it would not be grace, but chaos. Likewise, truth, if it were separated from grace, would not be truth, but cruelty. And as we pray in the Divine Liturgy, "You have not left me in need of any of the works of Your honor."[15]

Adam and Eve were enjoying God's grace. God created man on the sixth day after He had prepared everything for him, and as the Scripture says, "Who gives us richly all things to enjoy."[16] So, who is man? He is dust. So can I say that he was placed in paradise as a reward for his goodness? Of course not. It is God's grace which placed him in paradise. And because grace and truth are inseparable, God gave Adam a commandment, "Of every tree of the garden you may freely eat; but of the tree of the knowledge of good and evil you shall not eat, for in the day that you eat of it you shall surely die."[17] And Adam fell into disobeying God, and lost his relationship with God. Adam and Eve felt guilty and were ashamed

---

15   Divine Liturgy According to St. Gregory – Agios (Holy).

16   1 Timothy 16:17.

17   Genesis 2:16–17.

of themselves, and this shame is the opposite of the sense of safety [which is] present in God's grace.

And after the fall, God began putting in place a plan for man's salvation, as we pray in the Divine Liturgy, "You have not abandoned us to the end."[18] Therefore, He gave man truth, and truth is the Law which says, "Do this and you shall live,"[19] and because there was enmity between man and God, the relationship was not restored, because there was truth without there being grace. And the Law revealed the faults of man, and it was like a mirror revealing his faults. The Law said, for example, "Do not steal;" thereby I learned that when I steal, I am not faithful. Therefore, Scripture says, "Therefore the law was our tutor to bring us to Christ."[20]

The commandment restricted somewhat the evil which existed in man, but it did not restore the image of man, because had the Law been able to restore the image of man, there would not have been a need for the coming of Christ; "for if righteousness comes through the law, then Christ died in vain."[21] And by the Law man discovered his inability to keep the commandment, and consequently, he announced his need for grace, for without grace man cannot keep the commandment. Truth revealed to man that he is a sinner and deserving of death and the curse. And

---

18   Divine Liturgy According to St. Basil – Agios (Holy).

19   See Deuteronomy 4:1, 8:1, 30:16.

20   Galatians 3:24.

21   Galatians 2:21.

this is what usually happens with the person who is raised in a [Church] service that deals with truth [only], without the availability of an atmosphere of acceptance and love. St. Paul the Apostle says, "Because the law brings about wrath; for where there is no law there is no transgression."[22]

A person becomes rebellious in systems that lack grace, love, and acceptance, and that are based solely on [giving] orders. Consequently, deviations occur, and a sense of failure and ineptitude takes control. Therefore, grace and truth have to be present together, so that the human being may grow in a sound way. As we have previously said, if we separated truth from grace, it would be judgment; and if we separated grace from truth, it would be chaos. Therefore, Paul the Apostle says, "Stand fast therefore in the liberty by which Christ has made us free ... For you, brethren, have been called to liberty; only do not use liberty as an opportunity for the flesh."[23]

This is the faith of our Church. It does not separate grace from truth, does not separate faith from works, because faith without works is dead, as the Scripture says, "Thus also faith by itself, if it does not have works, is dead."[24] Works without faith cannot save the person. And grace we receive when we accept Christ.

---

22   Romans 4:15.

23   Galatians 5:1,13.

24   James 2:17.

The Lord Christ has granted us His grace without charge. He died on the cross, and accepted us and we were [still] sinners. And He gave us truth in the commandment, so if we break the commandment, His Blood on the altar grants us forgiveness. And He gave us the Holy Spirit who grants us help, so that we may keep the commandment.

The wages of sin is death[25], but the Lord through His grace granted us His Body which gives life and resurrection from the dead. And through His grace, man was reconciled with God, was reconciled with himself, and was reconciled with others. And the sense of safety returned, and the image, distorted by sin, was restored to the image of Christ, that we may be conformed to the image of His Son[26]. This is what St. Athanasius the Apostolic focused on in On the Incarnation.

The distorted image of man was restored in an atmosphere of grace, acceptance and truth. This atmosphere of grace changes the person. And this is the difference between Christian and secular counseling.

Secular counseling sometimes offers grace only, without biblical truth. So if a person were living in sin or were practicing homosexual relations, he would go to a counselor, who would help him accept himself, without clarifying to him biblical truth.

---

25   See Romans 6:23.

26   See Romans 8:29.

Christian counseling, however, offers him grace and truth together. And this is what we [exactly] see in the story of the woman caught in the very act. The Jews were judging her based on truth, and said, "That such should be stoned."[27] The Lord Christ, however, looked at her as a human being who needed acceptance, so He said to them, "He who is without sin among you, let him throw a stone at her first."[28] Yes, the commandment actually says "That such should be stoned," so the Lord Christ said, "Yes, stone her," because Christ will not alter the commandment, but in order to stone her, you must be without sin; therefore, they all left, and one Person remained, who was actually without sin. It was His right, Him alone, to stone her, because He is the Judge of the whole earth. But He looked at her and said, "'Woman, where are those accusers of yours? Has no one condemned you?' She said, 'No one, Lord.' And Jesus said to her, 'Neither do I condemn you; go and sin no more'"[29]

These words were the words of grace, because the time is not time for condemnation, but it is time for salvation. The Lord Christ granted her love, acceptance and forgiveness, though she is undeserving of these. But this is grace. He offered her, however, truth as well, in the form of a commandment, "Go and sin no more." Here are

---

27   John 8:5.

28   John 8:7.

29   John 8:10–11.

grace and truth together.

Therefore, God commanded us to stand in His presence with our true selves and not our feigned selves. Someone, for example, while feeling like reproving God for something, yet stands and prays, saying, "Lord, I thank You for everything, concerning everything, and in everything." And he might repeat words he has committed to memory, that do not express the truth of himself. David was accustomed to stand before God with his true self, and used to say to Him, for example, "How long, O Lord? Will You forget me forever? How long will You hide Your face from me?"[30] He would reveal himself to God, and God deals with the true self with His grace. Therefore, all the psalms that began with reproof of God, ended with thanksgiving and praising Him.

You have to reveal yourself, as it truly is, before God, because "God is Spirit, and those who worship Him must worship in spirit and truth."[31] And we serve God in spirit and truth. We stand before God without any embellishment; we stand before God with our blemishes and weaknesses, without making ourselves appear beautiful.

This is [exactly] what should take place in the Mystery of Confession. But sometimes when someone is confessing, he makes sure to justify

---

30   Psalm 13:1.
31   John 4:24.

his sin and makes it seem better. And it is [placed] upon the priest to realize that it is a sin. I have to show myself as it truly is before God, and when this happens, God unites with me on the spiritual level. This union is a grace from God, and consequently, I change.[32] When we take off the mask covering our faces in the Mystery of Confession, and we reveal ourselves as they truly are, God then gives us healing and deals with us with His grace, and we taste His love and grace, and we feel that we are His beloved and that we do not deserve this love. This union changes the person "into the same image from glory to glory."[33]

Growth does not only mean that a person unites with God, but he unites with his brother also; therefore, any member in the body is considered united with the head and the rest of the members.

Therefore, when they asked the Lord Christ:

"Which is the first commandment of all?" Jesus answered him, "The first of all the commandments is: 'Hear, O Israel, the LORD our God, the LORD is one. And you shall love the LORD your God with all your heart, with all your soul, with all your mind, and with all your strength.' This is the first commandment. And the second, like

---

32 Literally: my soul changes.

33 2 Corinthians 3:18.

it, is this: 'You shall love your neighbor as yourself.'"[34]

Let us note that the one who asked the Lord, asked Him for a *single* commandment, but the Lord Christ gave him two commandments. Growth requires union with the root, and also union with the rest of the members. Paul the Apostle explained this matter, saying, "...the Head, from whom all the body, nourished and knit together by joints and ligaments, grows with the increase that is from God."[35] The more a soul is united with God and united with others, on the level of grace and truth, the greater the growth of this person is.

Counselors and psychiatrists see that one of the best things that help in treating addicts, is living in groups, because if we gave the addicted person advice and spoke to him about the danger of addiction and its effects, this means that we are offering him truth and asking him to stay away from addiction. Indeed, he may respond for a short while, and may attempt [to do so], but in the end he would go back to addiction once again. In groups, on the other hand, a person feels the love, acceptance and unconditional tolerance. These groups offer truth as well.

The first step of the steps [used] in the groups for

---

34   Mark 12:28–31.

35   Colossians 2:19.

treatment of addiction, which consist in twelve steps, begins with the addict confessing his powerlessness and failure. And here he can be victorious over addiction. And in this atmosphere filled with love, acceptance and tolerance, he is permitted to enter into a loving relationship with God, on the level of grace and truth. Truth is the revealing of oneself, so he confesses that he is weak, and would not feign otherwise; and in grace, God shows acceptance, love and tolerance, and the addict experiences this with others with whom he is living.

Therefore, it is very important that we deal, in our relationship with God and others, on the level of truth, by our true selves and not the feigned. We should not put on the façade of righteousness when we stand before God, because whenever we put this façade on, we fail to change and our healing is obstructed.

And this is, [namely], the advice Paul the Apostle offers the Ephesians, "Therefore, putting away lying, 'Let each one of you speak truth with his neighbor,' for we are members of one another."[36]

Lying means that you hide who you truly are and your faults. And whenever we hide our faults, we fail, and it becomes difficult for us to heal. This façade which the fake person[37] puts on, immediately separates this person from grace and truth, and he

---

36   Ephesians 4:25.
37   Literally: soul or self.

remains isolated from them, and he suffers defeat and failure.

The first thing Adam and Eve did after the sin, is hiding from God, and they hid themselves by [using] fig leaves. But whenever a person submits[38] himself to grace and truth, he receives healing. Therefore, when they brought the paralytic to the Lord Christ, the Lord of glory looked at him and said to him, "Your sins are forgiven."[39] There were some people who did not like these words, for they were seeking for him healing [only], because, in their view, there was no room now for the forgiveness of sin. But the Lord asked them, [saying], "Which is easier, to say to the paralytic, 'Your sins are forgiven you,' or to say, 'Arise, take up your bed and walk'?"[40]

Perhaps, at first glance, we may think and say that "your sins are forgiven you" is easier, but "arise, take up your bed and walk" is a miracle—a paralytic rising and carrying his bed. The truth, however, is that "arise, take up your bed and walk" did not cost the Lord anything. Raising Lazarus from the dead did not cost Him anything. "Your sins are forgiven you," however, did cost the Lord, that He "made Himself of no reputation, taking the form of a bondservant, and coming in the likeness of men. And being found in appearance as a man, He

---

38   Or: presents, shows, exposes.

39   Mark 2:5.

40   Mark 2:9.

humbled Himself and became obedient to the point of death, even the death of the cross."[41]

Therefore, every time I confess, and the priest reads the absolution and puts the cross on my head, the price of this absolution is exceedingly great—its price is the blood of Christ, of which I am utterly unworthy. Rather, it is grace from Christ: "Knowing that you were not redeemed with corruptible things, like silver or gold, from your aimless conduct received by tradition from your fathers, but with the precious blood of Christ, as of a lamb without blemish and without spot."[42] In the Mystery of Confession, I expose myself to grace, but at the same time I find truth in the form of repentance, spiritual practices and spiritual canon, which I must pursue for the healing of my soul.

Fear, humiliation and shame are hindrances to spiritual growth and maturity. But if we confess our spiritual neediness and poverty, and we come to the grace of God to be enriched, we will receive a blessing: "Blessed are the poor in spirit, for theirs is the kingdom of heaven."[43] In the Book of Revelation, the Lord Christ says to the angel of the church of the Laodiceans, "Because you say, 'I am rich, have become wealthy, and have need of nothing' [that is, he cannot confess his sins]—and do not know that you are wretched, miserable, poor, blind, and

---

41 Philippians 2:7–8.

42 1 Peter 1:18–19.

43 Matthew 5:3.

naked."[44]

> *"Be ashamed when you sin, but do not be ashamed when you repent, for sin is the wound, and repentance is the treatment. Sin is followed by shame, and repentance is followed by boldness. But the devil has reversed this order, so he gives boldness in sin, and shame of repentance."*

—St. John Chrysostom—

Time

We have explained the factors of grace and truth, because, as we said, we should not separate them, for they are bound together.

As to the third factor, it is "time." Here we point to the parable which the Lord mentioned in the Gospel according to St. Luke:

> He also spoke this parable: "A certain man had a fig tree planted in his vineyard, and he came seeking fruit on it and found none. Then he said to the keeper of his vineyard, 'Look, for three years I have come seeking fruit on this fig tree and find none. Cut it down; why does it use up the ground?'

---

44   Revelation 3:17.

But he answered and said to him, 'Sir, let it alone this year also, until I dig around it and fertilize it. And if it bears fruit, well. But if not, after that you can cut it down.'"[45]

This parable speaks about someone who had a vineyard wherein was a fig tree, and for three years he found no fruit on it, so he decided to cut it down. This is what we sometimes do. When I look at myself and find no fruit, but only family and work problems, with the children and with friends, and consequently I judge myself a failure. And I ask [myself], "What is the point of my life? I suffer from anger, depression and stress." And in the end I may say, "Cut it down; why does it use up the ground? So what could I do more than that?" And then I fall into indifference.

But the keeper of the vineyard had wisdom. He saw that there was a third factor for the growth of the tree, in order that it may bring forth fruit: it is the factor of time. So he said, "Let it alone this year also," but the factor of time alone will not [cause it to] bring forth fruit, for the year might pass, without there being fruit on it too. Therefore, the keeper of the vineyard will do two things: the first thing is to "dig around it," that is, to pull out the weeds surrounding it which hinder growth; and the second thing is to "fertilize it," that is, to nourish it, which is steadfastness in grace. And we,

---

45   Luke 13:6–9.

sometimes, "tolerate" our children, and say, "I have been patient for long, and have tried diligently, but there is no fruit; therefore, I will kick him out of the house." And this is what sometimes happens in Sunday school classes. There may not be fruit, so we drive the child out of church. We ban him or drive him out.

The important question, however, is: Did we give this tree sufficient time, to dig around it and fertilize it, so that truth, which is the divine commandment, may cleanse this soul from lying, cheating and deception, and so that grace may supply this person with spiritual nourishment, love and holy, pure relationships, which make him according to the image of God? All these need time.

Paul the Apostle says to the Hebrews, "For though by this time you ought to be teachers."[46] That is to say, they were supposed to be teachers and bear fruit. Nevertheless, Paul the Apostle did not say, "Cut it down because there is no benefit hoped for from the Hebrews." And he did not ask for this church to be shut. Rather he said to them, "I will begin with you from the start, there is another time [yet]; therefore, I will feed you milk until you grow." "You need someone to teach you again the first principles of the oracles of God; and you have come to need milk."[47] He dug around it, looked

---

46   Hebrews 5:12.
47   Ibid.

into the problems present in the church, and put fertilizer, and with time it would bring forth fruit.

After Adam and Eve had fallen, God put in place a cherubim to guard the Tree of Life, so that they may not eat of it, because had they eaten, they would have continued in sin and the separation from God to the end; therefore, God guarded the Tree. Then was the judgment of sin: "Man shall surely die;" that is, "Cut it down now; why does it use up the ground?" That's how sin cried, but God said, "Leave it alone; there will be a time of visitation, and in that time I will redeem them by my grace, and cleanse them by truth. And so, they will change, grow, and become conformed to the image of My Son."

The time in which we live now, is not a time for judgment, but a time for redemption and salvation; therefore, in our homes and churches, we should not judge, condemn, cut down nor separate, and say, "Why does it use up the ground? Cut it down now." If our time had been a time for judgment, the Lord Christ would have judged the woman caught in the very act.

The Church reminds us in every Divine Liturgy: "He has appointed a Day for recompense, on which He will appear to judge the world in righteousness."[48] This means that the Lord Christ will come on a day for judgment[49], but the time in which He came was

---

48   The Divine Liturgy According to St. Basil – Agios (Holy).

49   Or: condemnation.

not for judgment[50], for He said, "For God did not send His Son into the world to condemn the world, but that the world through Him might be saved."[51]

James and John said to the Lord Christ when a Samaritan village rejected Him, "'Lord, do You want us to command fire to come down from heaven and consume them, just as Elijah did?' But He turned, rebuked them and said, 'You do not know what manner of spirit you are of. For the Son of Man did not come to destroy men's lives but to save them.'"[52] Unfortunately, we as fathers and mothers forget this and deal with this [present] time as though it were the time of judgment.

When the Lord sat down in the feast which Matthew prepared and to which he invited many tax collectors and others, the scribes and Pharisees complained and said to them, "How is it that your Teacher eat with the tax collectors and sinners?" because they did not care about the salvation of those sinners. But the Lord Christ said to them, "I have not come to call the righteous, but sinners, to repentance."[53] The Lord Christ came to treat humanity, so He sent the human soul into the operation room of time, so that He may transfer to it the blood of life, grace and nourishment, and that He may excise the tumors of sin. As Paul the

---

50   Ibid.
51   John 3:17.
52   Luke 9:54–56.
53   Luke 5:32.

Apostle says, "That He might present her to Himself a glorious church, not having spot or wrinkle or any such thing, but that she should be holy and without blemish."[54]

Sometimes there may be people who refuse to go into this operation room; therefore, the Lord weeps over them, as He wept over Jerusalem, because it did not know the time of its visitation[55]. Paul the Apostle realized the importance of the time of visitation and salvation, and this [present] time will end at some [point in] time; therefore, he said, "See then that you walk circumspectly, not as fools but as wise, redeeming the time, because the days are evil."[56]

We have to realize the importance of the time in which we are living, so that we do not waste days and years, and have to submits ourselves to grace and truth, until we have removed all the obstacles of growth, because the time of visitation will end and the door will be shut, and we will suddenly find ourselves before the judgment. Time for each person is the present moment, because he cannot ensure the next moment; therefore, Paul the Apostle says, "And do this, knowing the time, that now it is high time to awake out of sleep."[57]

---

54   Ephesians 5:27.

55   See Luke 19:44.

56   Ephesians 5:15–16.

57   Romans 13:11.

Growth and healing need time. But we have to work during this time earnestly, as the farmer does. He plants the seed in time, then waters his crop in time, and harvests in time. Sometimes we have no patience, so we want to harvest right away, without waiting for the [proper] time. We, too, should not hasten the time of harvest, but should plant, water, and remove harmful weeds, and necessarily time of harvest will come, for as Scripture says, "To everything there is a season, a time for every purpose under heaven."[58]

There were extremely difficult problems in the church which was in Corinth, wherein were divisions and strife, and nevertheless, Paul the Apostle did not say, "Cut it down; why does it use up the ground?" but said to them in the first epistle, "And I, brethren, could not speak to you as to spiritual people but as to carnal, as to babes in Christ. I fed you with milk and not with solid food; for until now you were not able to receive it, and even now you are still not able; for you are still carnal. For where there are envy, strife, and divisions among you, are you not carnal and behaving like mere men?"[59] The Apostle fed them with milk, and this is grace, so that they may grow and know right from wrong. And the Apostle was joyful when he saw the fruit of repentance in the Corinthian church.

---

58   Ecclesiastes 3:1.
59   1 Corinthians 3:1–3.

And in the Gospel of John, we read that the brothers of Christ—who were His cousins—told Him to go to Jerusalem to show Himself, so He said to them, "My time has not yet come, but your time is always ready."[60]

Growth happens gradually, and needs time, effort, toil, and struggle, but the devil often offers quick solutions, like what he did with the Lord Christ when He became hungry, and he asked Him to transform the stones into bread. The Lord Christ refused, because this is not the way with which He is satisfied [with bread]. And when he said to Him, "Throw Yourself down. For it is written: 'He shall give His angels charge over you,' and, 'In their hands they shall bear you up, lest you dash your foot against a stone.'"[61] So the Lord Christ refused, because He does not want this form of glory, for His glory is through the cross. Also, when the devil said to Him, "I will give You all the kingdoms of the world and their glory if You fall down and worship me."[62] So the Lord Christ drove him out and said to him, "I will become King, but I will reign upon the wood of the cross." The Lord Christ is as though saying to the devil, "My people, glory, and kingdom will be at a particular time, and not through quick solutions. They will be through the narrow gate and struggle."

60   John 7:6.

61   Matthew 4:6.

62   Cf. Matthew 4:8–9.

Quick solutions sometimes lead to failure. Growth and success, however, need time. The devil might come to a young man who has recently graduated from university, and whispers to him that the road is difficult and obstructed, and that his future is uncertain. Consequently, this young man pursues to be rich quickly, and proceeds on the road of unfaithfulness, but he falls in the end. The Holy Scripture says, "A faithful man will abound with blessings, but he who hastens to be rich will not go unpunished."[63]

Likewise, the devil may approach an adolescent young man, and entice him into satisfying his flesh by way of sensual pleasure, but the Lord says to him, "Wait until you are in a godly relationship through the Mystery of Matrimony. Then you will find perfect satisfaction."

Sometimes a person may encounter problems in his life, so the devil would entice him into drinking alcohol or taking drugs, to run away from these problems, but the Lord asks him to cling to Him and promises to build in him a strong personality which is able to endure these problems and overcome them.

In the parable of the sower which the Lord Christ mentioned, some seed fell on stony places, where they did not have enough earth and where no one dug around them. They sprang up quickly,

---

63   Proverbs 28:20.

but when the sun was up they were scorched.[64] And so, quick solutions usually lead to many years of suffering.

Growth and change take time, but of the wonderful things is that the person does not know how growth takes place. The Lord Christ spoke about the changes that happen in the life of a person, and mentioned the following parable. "The kingdom of God is as if a man should scatter seed on the ground, and should sleep by night and rise by day, and the seed should sprout and grow, he himself does not know how. For the earth yields crops by itself: first the blade, then the head, after that the full grain in the head."[65] The statement "he himself does not know how," means that when a person places himself under grace, and with divine truth, he will grow and change, yet he himself does not know how; but he has to begin now. He should reveal himself as he truly is, and should not do like the unprofitable servant who took the talent and hid it.[66] This talent is his soul. For if the person does not reveal himself in the grace and truth of Christ, he will not change.

Growth, as we have previously said, requires time, effort, and struggle; therefore, our teacher James says, "My brethren, count it all joy when

---

64   See Matthew 13:5.

65   Mark 4:26–28.

66   See Matthew 25:25.

you fall into various trials."[67] If you are suffering from a trial, which you are going through because of [your] upbringing and education, and if you endure this suffering with the true self and you expose it to the light of the grace of Christ, then Scripture says to you, "That you may be perfect and complete, lacking nothing."[68] The following will take place: your true self will grow and become complete and lacking nothing, through this suffering.

As for the grumbling soul, which is not joyful [but] is always complaining about its upbringing in such a home, it will not grow nor be healed.

Perhaps some might ask, "Was there no grace in the Old Testament?!" There was, undoubtedly, grace in God's dealings with man. Grace was manifested in God's dealings with Abraham when he lied, and was also manifested [in God's dealing] with the people of Nineveh, and in numerous other examples. But when we speak about grace in the New Testament, we are talking about the salvific grace, which saved man from sin, and opened the gate of paradise and restored man to it.[69] God is not able to separate grace from truth in Himself, for they exist [together] in Him, but concerning salvation, this grace is in the Lord Christ, as Paul the Apostle said, "For the grace of God that brings salvation has appeared

---

67   James 1:2.

68   James 1:4.

69   See Sunday Theotokia – Part 15.

to all men."[70] This grace that bring salvation has appeared in the incarnation of the Lord Christ and His death upon the cross; therefore, we should not mix between this grace which appeared in Christ and the grace of God's dealing with people.

> *"Do not say, 'I have kept the commandments but have not found the Lord.'... 'Those who rightly seek him will find peace.[71] Peace is the deliverance from the passions. Peace, as the holy Apostle says, is not found except through the workings of the Holy Spirit[72]."[73]*
>
> —Mark the Ascetic—

---

70   Titus 2:11.

71   Proverbs 16:8 LXX.

72   Romans 8:2,6.

73   Mark the Monk, *Counsels on the Spiritual Life*, T. Vivian and A. Casiday, trans. (Crestwood, NY: St. Vladimir's Seminary Press, 2009), 110.

2

Characteristics of the Mature Person

There are four characteristics of a person who has changed into the image of God, and these are:

✤ Mastering how to bond and establish a relationship with others, whether the other is God, a father or mother, a brother or sister, a friend, husband or a wife.

✤ Mastering, too, how to separate from others in a sound way, when they enter university or when they form a new family, so they separate from the parents and leave their parents' house.

✤ Mastering how to discriminate between good and evil, and this discrimination between good and evil is one of the marks of maturity.

✤ Mastering how to bear responsibility, thereby

becoming mature persons.

Many ask, "How do I establish a true relationship with God?" When God created man, he created him a relational being who grows through relationships. Therefore, the ability to bond with others is a true psychological need. If this bonding were not present, the person may suffer from depression. Therefore, God said, "It is not good that man should be alone."[74]

An experiment was done on children who were raised in isolation from others, and they provided for them all their bodily needs of food and drink, but there was no one there to carry them [in their arms], hug them, talk with them, nor establish a relationship with them. So what happened? They all died at the age of three or four years. From this true experiment, we can conclude that, for the human being[75] to grow, he needs food and drink, and needs, too, to enter into a relationship with God and another [human being].

This applies to plants too. For example, if we cut a branch off and separate it from the tree, it dies. But for it to bear fruit, it must be bound to the tree, and this is what the Lord Christ said, "He who abides in Me, and I in him, bears much fruit; for without Me you can do nothing. If anyone does not abide in Me, he is cast out as a branch and is

---

74 Genesis 2:18.
75 Literally: soul.

withered."[76] Therefore, He said after these words, "This is My commandment, that you love one another as I have loved you."[77] As long as the person is in a relationship with the Lord Christ, and in a relationship with others, he grows and bears much fruit.

God Himself is Trinity; that is, in Him there is a loving relationship between the three Hypostases. In the Book of Genesis, it says that we were created in the image of God. And this means that we were created as relational beings, because in God too there is a relationship between the Holy Trinity. He says in the Gospel of our teacher John, "He who does not love Me does not keep My words; and the word which you hear is not Mine but the Father's who sent Me."[78] This confirms that there is a relationship between the Son and the Father. And He also says, "I do not pray for these alone, but also for those who will believe in Me through their word; that they all may be one, as You, Father, are in Me, and I in You; that they also may be one in Us, that the world may believe that You sent Me. And the glory which You gave Me I have given them, that they may be one just as We are one: I in them, and You in Me; that they may be made perfect in one, and that the world may know that You have sent Me, and have loved

---

76   John 15:5–6.

77   John 15:12.

78   John 14:24.

them as You have loved Me."[79]

And in his first epistle, John the Apostle says, "God is love, and he who abides in love abides in God, and God in him."[80]

And how is love practiced? Love is always symbolized by the number 2, because love is between two [people], and it is practiced through relationships. Consequently, relationships and bonding are a foundational condition for the growth of the human being, because, by being in a relationship with God and with others, the person will experience love, and love facilitates growth.

When the Lord Christ was asked, "What is the greatest commandment?"—and for Him, the commandment is truth, because truth is what regulates relationships—He, therefore, said that the greatest truth is that you shall love the Lord your God... shall love your neighbor as yourself.[81] For when we say "reveal yourself to truth" or "live by truth," we mean that you submit yourself to living with love, which is grace. Therefore, I have previously said that it is difficult for a person to separate between truth and grace. Submitting to truth is living with love, because keeping the commandment of truth means that a person lives with love for God and for others. The goal of all the

---

79   John 17:20–23.

80   1 John 4:16.

81   See Luke 10:27.

commandments which God has given us is to love God and love others, because when I love God and love my brother, I will grow and change into that divine image.

Sometimes some people think that they have to be perfect first, and [only] then will they love God and their brothers, while the opposite is true. For by keeping the commandment, we learn how to love God and how to love our brothers, and, so, we will grow and change to be conformed to the divine image. Therefore, the person will remain untrue until he has learned how to bond with God and others.

Let us contemplate that beautiful image which Paul the Apostle mentioned in his epistle to the Ephesians: "That you, being rooted and grounded in love, may be able to comprehend with all the saints what is the width and length and depth and height—to know the love of Christ which passes knowledge; that you may be filled with all the fullness of God."[82] Two things Paul the Apostle mentions in this verse, "rooted" and "grounded." Rooted is [like] the root of a plant, and grounded is like the foundation of a house. The Apostle here is saying, as a tree has a root, and as a building has a foundation, so love is the root and foundation upon which our life is built. And when you are rooted and grounded in love, you may be able to comprehend

---

82   Ephesians 3:17–19.

with all the saints, through your connection[83] with the fellowship of the church, what is the width and length and depth and height. Therefore, we pray in the Divine Liturgy, "He made us unto Himself an assembled people, and sanctified us by Your Holy Spirit,"[84] and the mysteries of the kingdom of heaven shall be revealed to you, too, and you shall know the love of Christ which passes knowledge.

The Apostle then says this powerful and very stunning verse, "That you may be filled with all the fullness of God."[85] This is the growth I would like to attain. So how can I be a successful person, and be conformed to the image of His Son? I cannot attain this unless I am rooted and grounded in love. And this is your relationship with God and others. Falling into sin cuts off man's relationship with God, and man's relationship with others, too, and no longer does man love his brother.

> *"You have known God; this is much better. I wish that you grow in this knowledge. And let each passing day bring you closer—even closer—to God."*
>
> —H.H. Pope Shenouda III—

---

83   Literally: relationship.

84   The Divine Liturgy According to St. Basil – Agios (Holy).

85   Ephesians 3:19.

Therefore, we have seen something puzzling: though Cain had not seen any creature getting killed, nor had he seen anyone die, but because he parted from love and from God, he rose up against his brother Abel, and killed him; and [so] pain and suffering went into man's life, because a relationship was no longer present. And man became rebellious against God and against his brother, and our image became distorted because of the fall, so man is no longer in the image of God. Therefore, the Redeemer came, to reconcile man with God, and to reconcile man with others. The goal of redemption was to restore man to the image of God, which he lost through the fall, and this, through reconciliation. And this is meaning which Paul the Apostle summarized in the first chapter of the epistle to the Colossians, and he said, "For it pleased the Father that in Him all the fullness should dwell, and by Him [that is, by Christ] to reconcile all things to Himself, by Him, whether things on earth or things in heaven, having made peace through the blood of His cross. And you, who once were alienated and enemies in your mind by wicked works, yet now He has reconciled in the body of His flesh through death, to present you holy, and blameless, and above reproach in His sight."[86] Here God describes man's works that they are wicked, and his image distorted, but He has reconciled us in the body of His flesh through death, and brought us with Him, and with

---

86   Colossians 1:19–22.

others, into a true relationship of love, to present us holy, and blameless, and above reproach in His sight.

If you want to change and eliminate the problems which you have encountered because of your upbringing, enter into a loving relationship with God and others [in your life], and these problems will be resolved. When I learn how to love God, and train myself to love my brother, I will change and become conformed to the image of His Son.

The whole message of the gospel is the restoration of the relationship and bond with God and with others. And the relationship with God and others will not be formed automatically, because we live in a fallen, corrupt world, polluted by sin. Therefore, it is important that I strive to remain steadfast in my relationship with God and my relationship with others. And without bonding and forming this relationship, not only will the person stop growing, but he will regress, [also,] and his psychological and spiritual state will deteriorate.

Most psychological problems, including the difficult ones like addiction, may be eliminated through relationships. For healthy and spiritual relationships contain love and acceptance, grace and truth. And this is the theological and biblical side for the importance of bonding with others. And even on the psychological level, psychiatrists declare the same thing. An embryo, in its mother's womb, experiences bonding with the mother, and then it has a sense of safety. And when [the baby] is born, coming out of his mother's womb, he experiences a shock because he was separated from her; and when he feels separated and alienated from the mother, he screams and begins crying, for he feels unsafe, because he used to receive blood, was nourished, and felt a warmth while in the mother's womb. [Yet] from there, he came out into the world. Therefore, the mother carries her newborn son, embraces him, caresses him, offers him love and affection while she breastfeeds him, so the baby begins bonding with his mother, and this makes him feel safe, psychologically, and gives him plenty of safety. And he learns that he is loved, because all carry him in their arms, hug him, give him kisses, and play with him.

The plenty of love and safety which a baby receives, helps him to stay away, a little, from his mother, and he runs and plays [on his own]. And after a year or two, he is able to enter into relationships with other children and to love them. But the baby who has not felt this love, tenderness, and safety, you will find that he screams whenever he is away from his mother. As for the loved baby, when he reaches the age of three years, he can play at a distance, and go to the playground in the church's yard or any other safe place, and can play without fear or disturbance.

And this is the feeling of safety and love, which

makes a mature man form a loving relationship with his wife. He could go to his office at work, shut his door behind him, and remain alone, away from his wife, without having a sense of loneliness or homesickness. But if the person did not feel safe, he would feel that he is a stranger, anxious, and lonely, while being even with his wife, for example. Such experiences may be had with God, also.

The parents who always make their children scared of God—for example they may say to them, "If you lie, God will throw you in hell," "If you do this, God will be angry with you," "Jesus is angry with you," or "Jesus is frowning because you did so,"—[through] such words, they distort God's image in our children's mind, even though Paul the Apostle says, "But God demonstrates His own love toward us, in that while we were still sinners, Christ died for us."[87]

But if I know for certain that I am loved by God and am His son, and that He loves me, not because I am good, but because He is good and His mercy endures forever, then this will grant me a sense of spiritual safety. And I know that I love God, and He will not reject me; therefore, I live in peace which surpasses all understanding[88]. Parents should not distort God's image in their children's mind, because God is love and loves us with an everlasting

---

87   Romans 5:8.

88   See Philippians 4:7.

love; therefore, He says, "I have loved you with an everlasting love; therefore with lovingkindness I have drawn you."[89] And therefore a person can enter into a relationship with God, because he feels that God loves him.

If we asked anyone why they have not entered into a true relationship with God, they might answer, "Because I am a sinful person," which makes him feel that he is rejected by God. But if he realized that God loves him, he would enter into a relationship with Him, and then he would change and forsake sin, as it happened with the Samaritan woman. When this woman entered into a relationship with the Lord Christ and felt His love, she was changed, left her waterpot, and became a preacher.[90]

When a sense of safety and love is formed in the child, he will have the confidence that pushes him to form successful friendships and relationships with others. And these friendships with others would increase his sense of safety, and when the sense of safety increases, [in turn], the person enters into more relationships, and so on, until he is a young man, so he goes into university or gets a job. And sometimes he is compelled, because of school, work or marriage, to separate from his family, and this separation would be sound, without there being any psychological problems.

---

89   Jeremiah 31:3.
90   See John 4.

Research was done, once, on the importance of relationships with others, for the healing of bodily illnesses, like heart diseases. They discovered that the person who was surrounded with loved ones and friends, who offer him love, compassion, and tenderness, gained healing quickly, in contrast with the person who is lonely, who has no one to love him and support him. John the Apostle emphasized this idea, saying, "We know that we have passed from death to life, because we love the brethren."[91]

Forming a relationship with others has many benefits, of which we mention [the following] three:

✣ In the person is form a good foundation of values, morals, and principles.

✣ The person has a greater ability to deal with problems and the stresses of life.

✣ It gives the achievements he has accomplished in his life a meaning, value, and depth.

There may be a person who keeps the values, morals, and principles, from the standpoint of him being obliged to do so. And there is another person who keeps them, out of love. If you used to obey, for example, because you were obliged to do so, you would obey when the person, who had ordered this of you, is present, and would not obey in his absence. As for the one who obeys out of love, he may be [even] more obedient in the absence of the

---

91   1 John 3:14.

person than in his presence. And he who tries to acquire values, morals, and principles, away from love, will fail, because he whose heart is bonded with love, the fruit of values and morals will come naturally as a result of his love for God and others. St. Augustine says, "Love God, and do whatever you want." For the one who loves cannot hurt others' feelings, and if you love your brother, you will never lie to him, and will not hurt him, [rather] will be patient with him. A mother breast-feeds her baby and bears him [in her arms], not because she is obliged and it is her duty, but because he is her baby and she loves him. Even if she were tired and very exhausted, [when] she hears her baby cry in the middle of the night, she runs to him and makes sure that he is okay, because she loves him. There is a huge difference between visiting someone sick because you have to do so, and visiting a sick person because you love him.

All the works of the Lord Christ were preceded always by the words, "He had compassion." And this is what He did with the widow of Nain when He saw her weeping. The Scripture says, "When the Lord saw her, He had compassion on her and said to her, 'Do not weep.'"[92] [Then] He raised her son [from the dead].

Bonding with others helps the person, too, to face stresses and problems. We all face many

---

92   Luke 7:13.

problems, and need support—that is, for my brother to stand by me, as Paul the Apostle says, "Bear one another's burdens, and so fulfill the law of Christ."[93] The person who has not learned how to bond with others, will find it very difficult to say to someone that he is in need of others' help. In contrast to that is the person who has bonded with another. It is very easy for him to say that he needs your support, because he is going through a tough time.

The Lord Christ—glory be to Him—being God, when He was in the garden of Gethsemane, took Peter, James, and John with Him, to keep watch with Him because he was going through a tough time. And when they fell asleep, He reproved them, saying, "What! Could you not watch with Me one hour?"[94] It is as though the Lord Christ wanted to give us an example, that when we are facing a problem, there is nothing wrong in me saying to others, "Come and keep watch with me." And through bonding and the relationship with others, I can pass through the trial and destroy the stresses, and the problem would come to an end.

David the prophet went through many stressful circumstances in his life, but his friendship with Jonathan helped him very much face these stresses. And when Jonathan died, he lamented him with very beautiful words, sating, "I am distressed for you,

---

93   Galatians 6:2.
94   Matthew 26:40.

my brother Jonathan; you have been very pleasant to me; your love to me was wonderful, surpassing the love of women."[95] You have been very pleasant because you gave me much support, and stood by me when I was running away from your father, and you delivered me out of his hand.

Bonding with others gives meaning to our achievements and our success in life. And a person, through relationships, is able to accomplish greater achievements, and these achievements would have a profound meaning. If he had no relationships, however, neither would his life have a meaning. He may have exceedingly great amount of money, may occupy the loftiest posts and may attain a high position, yet there is an emptiness in his life which has no meaning. And we hear many say that they do not enjoy the warmth that is derived from relationships. The goal of work is not that I have a large balance in the bank, nor that I reach a high position, nor that I run away from problems by spending more time at work; rather, I work and attain success so that I may serve others. There are many who were successful in their life, [but] after they attained great success and occupied the loftiest posts, they abandoned them and established organizations working in serving humanity, like what president Carter did, who established an organization for serving those in need. And this is what Holy Scripture says, "As each one has received a gift, minister it to one another,

---

95   2 Samuel 1:26.

as good stewards of the manifold grace of God."[96]

What happens when a person, because of upbringing, fails in bonding with others, and is not able to form successful relationships? The person feels lonely, isolated, and estranged.

This isolation and estrangement passes through three stages:

The first stage [consists of] grumbling and distress, in which the person feels pain because he is alone, and feels that he is a stranger and has nobody to ask about him, and that nobody loves him. But he may [even] grumble against God, and say that the Lord does not love him, and may grumble against society wherein he lives. This person complains, because he has failed in making sound relationships. For this person to overcome this matter, he has to deal with this pain in a positive way, and from it, as an impetus, set out to form relationships and friendships with others, and then he can heal himself and grow in a sound way. If he does not do this, he will enter into the next stage.

The second stage is what we call, the building up of the feelings of grumbling against everything around him, because the feeling of the pain of loneliness persists for a long time. So you find him grumbling against God and others, and against home, church, and school.

---

96   1 Peter 4:10.

As for the third stage, it is the most dangerous, in which the person feels that he does not deserve to live, and then he ends his life and reaches the point of [committing] suicide.

From the aforementioned, the importance of forming relationships is made clear, and [also] bonding with God and entering into a relationship with God, so he will bask in the warmth of His love, and will attain success in his life, as Joseph bonded with God, and therefore, Scripture says, "The Lord was with Joseph, and he was a successful man."[97]

---

97   Genesis 39:2.

3

The Ability to Deal with the Good and the Bad

A truth we all must realize is that the world wherein we live includes good and bad together. Every person has the good, and has the bad too. There are points of strength and weakness, in the life of each of us. No one can claim, no matter who he is, that everything he has is good, and everything everyone else has is bad.

The problem lies in that some people who have not reached spiritual maturity yet, divide the world and people into [either] good or bad, but the matter may [even] reach to [the point] that a person may divide himself into what is good and what is bad. Such a person may lose the ability to deal with others, but [even] may lose the ability to deal with himself, in a true way and mature manner.

Such a perspective is, undoubtedly, incorrect, because this classification into, and separation between, good and bad, is far from reality and is untrue. This separation will not take place except in the last day, because the time in which we live now is a time of salvation and grace.

As a good example for this, let us go back, to about two thousand years ago, and let us imagine that we are living during the time of the Lord Christ. During this time, we happen to meet Judas and the right-hand thief. So, how will we separate one from the other? Judas was one of the twelve disciples, used to preach, perform miracles, and cast out demons, and consequently, we would place him in the good side. But the right-hand thief, we would place him in the bad side, and we might not know how to deal with him, because he is a bad and evil person. Let us, however, meditate on what will happen in the last day, when the Lord Christ sets the sheep on His right and the goats on His left, so where will each of Judas and the right-hand thief stand? Undoubtedly, the right-hand thief will stand with the saints and the righteous, but Judas will be with the wicked [men].

Separating the good from the evil makes the person incapable of dealing with others in the right and true way. If he puts it in his mind that this person is evil, then he will deal with him on [the basis] of him being a bad person. Even if this person began changing himself, he would think that the person is acting that way to deceive him, and would interpret his actions as bad. When we view any person with such a perspective, we judge him in our minds, and consequently, we head towards punishing him, and go as far as isolating him, and warn others about him so that no one would deal with him, nor come close to him. And if I failed in isolating him and warning people about him, then I would isolate myself from him.

This [same] description may be applied to departments and organizations. Someone might go to a [new] church, and after frequenting it for several months, he would say, "This church is bad and I will not go to it again. Its service is bad, there is no orderliness in it, but even everything in it is bad." Then he looks for another church, and classifies it as bad too. In the end, he separates himself from every church, because he will not find a perfect church on earth. Every church has flaws and weaknesses.

I read once a saying of an author, which included the following: "There is no perfect church, devoid of weaknesses and deficiencies, in this world. And if it so happened that we find a perfect church with no flaws in it, I advise that you should not go to it, because you are an imperfect person, and none of us is perfect; therefore, as soon as you enter it, this church will be imperfect, because of the presence of an imperfect person in it—that is, you."

And we sometimes isolate ourselves from others,

whom we have characterized as evil, or we isolate [ourselves] from church. Or perhaps a person may isolate himself from his job, when he is doing a work he does not like, and so he submits his resignation and looks for another job, and so he moves from work to work, and everywhere he goes he finds flaws only. Therefore, he keeps on saying that he has not found people who love him, and there is no fairness in this work, etc. And this person continues to search for perfection, and will not find it, for there is no absolute perfection on earth.

And [yet] there are some people who look at everything as good, and utterly deny the presence of evil. This perspective is unrealistic, too. They look at principles with a relative perspective, and so they say that all principles are good, and the principle which is [considered] good in a particular culture may not be so in another. And what is important is the culture in which this principle is applied.

Therefore, they say that right and wrong are relative matters. So, if the topic was about homosexuality, for example, they refer this to [the environment], that if the person grew up and was brought up in an environment that viewed this topic as wrong, then he would consider it wrong, but if the person was brought up in an environment that viewed this matter as irreproachable and sound, then he would consider it sound. And by this, they try to make [it appear that] everything is good, and there is nothing wrong with it.

And such [people] keep on also saying, "We cannot say about religions, that this religion is wrong and that religion is right, for all religions lead to God and to that Great Power. And even if you did not believe in the existence of God and that Great Power, your faith would be correct too." And this is some sort of "watering down" of principles, which makes people deal carelessly with them. For everything is right, and there is nothing wrong or bad, and consequently, it leads to extremely grave damages in [our] dealings.

The mature person is he who knows that the good and bad exist together and concurrently. For each of us harbors good and bad [things]. There is no organization or department devoid of correct and wrong things. If a person could perceive this truth, and act accordingly, then he has reached the stage of maturity, because he will deal with others in a realistic and true way, and [likewise deal] with the world, organizations, and departments. And this is what the Lord said in the parable of the wheat and the tares, "Let both grow together until the harvest."[98]

Before the fall, Holy Scripture says, "Then God saw everything that He had made, and indeed it was very good."[99] There was nothing evil before the fall, in man's world at least. And there was absolutely

---

98 Matthew 13:30.

99 Genesis 1:31.

nothing evil before the fall of the angels. The whole creation was good, and this is [exactly] what we pray in the Divine Liturgy, "O God, the Great, the Eternal, who formed man in incorruption."[100]

But through the fall, man knew good and evil, together. And the knowledge of evil began entering into man's life. And [now] he had to deal with good and bad, with good and evil, though he was created to deal with the good only, because he was created in incorruption. And because he was not suited to deal with [both] the good and bad, this made him characterize the things that are imperfect as evil and bad, and began forming an ideal image for everything: how the church should be and how a person must be?

Deep inside everyone there is an ideal image of how work, entities, organizations, countries, or even governments should be. And when he does not see this image present, he begins to say that this person is bad, or that country is bad, and so also he characterizes the church, and casts judgment upon everything and divides them into good and bad.

And because we were created in the image of God and His likeness, we know what the ideal characteristics are. And [yet] because the knowledge of good and evil has entered into man's life, then he knows that he is imperfect and has weaknesses, and

---

100   The Divine Liturgy According to St. Basil – Prayer of Reconciliation.

this thing creates a sort of conflict within the person between the ideal self and the true, realistic self. Paul the Apostle described this conflict in a very wonderful way when he said, "For what I am doing, I do not understand. For what I will to do, that I do not practice; but what I hate, that I do."[101] And in the thirty-first chapter of the Book of Proverbs, we read the characteristics of the virtuous woman, [yet] who in the whole world could say that all these characteristics are present in a woman, without she breaking any of them. And this creates a conflict between idealism and realism.

The same words could be applied to the characteristics of the ideal man, yet who could confidently say that all these characteristics of the ideal man are present in us?

This conflict may be good, if the person knew how to deal, in a sound way, with the good and bad which is in him. And this is what has brought about the natural yearning within a person, to pursue to be perfect, incorruptible, and without sin. Even atheists who basically do not believe in the existence of God, feel within themselves [the existence of] a conflict or yearning for a virtuous and ideal life, and they may ask about the meaning of life and its value, and about love and its importance. And psychologists say that this yearning, and this search for the meaning of life and love and virtuous principles, is nothing

---

101 Romans 7:15.

but a search for God. But what made the soul yearns in its depths for a virtuous life, perfect love, and good characteristics and principles, is that God is present within us, because we are created in the image of God. And this is what made St. Augustine say, "You have created us, O God, for Yourself, and our souls will remain anxious and perplexed until they rest in You."

Whether the person is a believer or unbeliever, he is created for God and in His image, and our souls will remain anxious and perplexed until they find rest in Him.

This yearning is a yearning for the first image in which we were created, and it will be realized in eternity, because there we will be without sin, and man will not fall into sin. And this is [also] what St. John said, "Whoever has been born of God does not sin, for His seed remains in him; and he cannot sin, because he has been born of God."[102] And this verse troubles people sometimes, because they may not be able to understand it: What does he mean by "Whoever has been born of God does not sin," for we have been born of God in Baptism and have received the guarantee of perfect adoption? We know that Jewish marriage used to be completed over three stages: the engagement stage, then a stage they called "betrothal," which is the equivalent of civil marriage, and the third stage which is the

---

102 1 John 3:9.

true marriage. The civil marriage is the lawful and official marriage, but the husband and wife do not practice the marital relationship. Our Lady Virgin [Mary's] bonding with St. Joseph was like this civil [marriage]; therefore, the angel said Joseph, "Do not be afraid to take to you Mary your wife."[103] The word "wife" here is correct, though he did not know her before nor after the birth of Christ, because she is the Ever-virgin; but there was [a marriage] that resembles the civil marriage.

But what is the connection between faith and marriage? Our relationship with Christ is that of marriage, for Christ is the Bridegroom. When Christ is preached to an unbeliever, Christ resembles a bridegroom. When He introduces Himself to a girl and she accepts Him, then the engagement is fulfilled. Faith resembles the engagement. And after faith and repentance, the second stage comes about, and civil marriage is performed which is completed in the Mystery of Baptism, "for as many of you as were baptized into Christ have put on Christ."[104] For we are transformed through Myron into a temple of the Holy Spirit, and through Communion, God abides in us, and we in Him. This resembles civil marriage. As for the perfect marriage, it will be fulfilled in the Second Coming of Christ, or when the soul departs from the body and goes to its Bridegroom. For this reason, this is described as marriage. And

---

103 Matthew 1:20.

104 Galatians 3:27.

this is what was said about the marriage supper of the Lamb in the Book of Revelation, and what Paul the Apostle mentioned also, "For I have betrothed you to one husband, that I may present you as a chaste virgin to Christ."[105] The word [used] here is "betrothed" and not "engaged." And consequently, we can say that we are granted adoption in Baptism and the Mysteries, and this resembles civil marriage.

Paul the Apostle says, "Not only that, but we also who have the firstfruits of the Spirit,—[that is, who have received the guarantee who is the Holy Spirit in Baptism and Myron]—even we ourselves groan within ourselves, eagerly waiting for the adoption, the redemption of our body."[106] We groan within ourselves, because we are still under sin and corruption, and the struggle between good and bad is still ongoing; therefore, we are eagerly waiting for the perfect adoption when our bodies arise, and we are completely given in marriage to our heavenly Bridegroom, the Lord Jesus. The clause "the redemption of our body" means the resurrection of bodies, and in that case man cannot sin [any longer], and all become good. And this is the explanation of the words of St. John, "Whoever has been born of God does not sin ... and he cannot sin."[107] And in this state we will be in eternity, when we receive perfect adoption by the redemption of the bodies in

---

105   2 Corinthians 11:2.

106   Romans 8:23.

107   1 John 3:9.

the general resurrection and the coming of Christ.

Paul the Apostle mentions, "For we know that the whole creation groans and labors with birth pangs together until now."[108] The groaning and the labor with birth pangs are a result of the struggle between the ideal self and the realistic self, between good and evil which exist within us and in the world too. And these good and evil do exist in the believers too; therefore, Paul the Apostle says, "Not only that, but we also who have the firstfruits of the Spirit."[109] We, the believers, groan too within ourselves, eagerly waiting for the redemption of our body. Paul the Apostle digresses, saying, "For we were saved in this hope, but hope that is seen is not hope; for why does one still hope for what he sees?"[110] He speaks, in this context, about a hope which we do not see now, but is something we eagerly wait for, and in this hope which we do not see, we were saved. And he says, "But if we hope for what we do not see, we eagerly wait for it with perseverance."[111] So this perfect adoption we eagerly wait for with perseverance, and therefore, the struggle between good and evil needs also perseverance. This struggle will continue, between the ideal self and the true self which is imperfect, for no one of us is perfect. One is perfect, and it is He who said, "Which of you

---

108 Romans 8:22.

109 Romans 8:23.

110 Romans 8:24.

111 Romans 8:25.

convicts Me of sin?"[112]

So long as we are in this world, and despite our constant pursuit of perfection—because the Lord commanded us saying, "You shall be perfect"[113]—no one could claim that he has attained perfection. This [likewise] is what Paul the Apostle says in his epistle to the Philippians[114], "Not that I have already attained, or am already perfected." This is to say, I cannot claim that I have attained this perfection, but I do the following. "But I press on," that is, I continue to press on and grow every day of my life, and why do I press on? "That I may lay hold of that for which Christ Jesus has also laid hold of me." That is, I press on that I may lay hold of that perfection and holiness, for which Christ Jesus has also laid hold of me, for He came down from heaven, was incarnate, became man, and died upon the cross, so as to give me holiness and perfection. "Brethren, I do not count myself to have apprehended." In case one of us might say that we are perfected, but I do not count myself to have apprehended. "But one thing I do, forgetting those things which are behind and reaching forward to those things which are ahead." That is, I forget the weaknesses and sin, and grow toward the life of perfection and holiness. "I press toward the goal," and the goal is to be perfect and holy, "for the prize of the upward call of God

---

112 John 8:46.

113 Matthew 5:48.

114 Philippians 3:12–15.

in Christ Jesus." Then he adds, "Therefore let us, as many as are mature[115], have this mind." What he means here by "as many as are mature," is those of you who think that they are perfect, or someone who thinks that he has nothing bad in him. And this is not true because no one is perfect. "And if in anything you think otherwise, God will reveal even this to you."[116] That is, God will reveal to him that there is no one who could say of himself that he is perfect upon the earth. And if we realized this mystery and truth, that no one is perfect, then we would walk according to this same law and keep in mind this same [law]. Therefore, my whole life becomes a struggle, "One thing I do, forgetting those things which are behind and reaching forward to those things which are ahead."[117]

> *"Your life with all its energy is a talent God has entrusted you with. Therefore you need to develop your personality, in general, that it may be transformed into a strong balanced personality, whether in the mind, or the conscience, or the will, or the knowledge, or the wisdom and the conduct, or the judgement of things, or the balanced temperament."*
>
> —H.H. Pope Shenouda III—

---

115 The word in the Arabic verse may be translated as "perfect."
116 Philippians 3:12–15.
117 Philippians 3:13.

4

The Ideal Self and the True Self

The struggle between the ideal self and the true self may take [one of] four forms, which we will talk about in details later.

The ideal self rejects the true self. When I know myself as it truly is, with its weaknesses, I reject this true self, forcing it to disappear. Therefore, it does not appear before anybody else, and consequently I appear with a feigned self[118] before others, and put on an appearance[119]. This appearance may be that of righteousness or hypocrisy. And when I form a relationship, whether with God or others, the one forming this relationship is the feigned self, and this feigned self cannot enter into a true relationship

---

118   Or: fake self.
119   Literally: mask.

with God or others, because it will be a feigned relationship.

To enter into a real relationship with God and with others, where there is a deep bond, I must enter into this relationship with my true self, and not the feigned self. And though I pursue perfection, I must too confess my weakness, and not hide it. I should not deny the truth of myself and my inability, because this denial makes people wonder, "How can a person become a Christian and a realist, at the same time?" A Christian is not perfect, and without sin, but he merely realizes that he has shortcomings and weaknesses. But the person who sees that a Christian must be perfect and without sin, and that a realist has weaknesses, consequently this realist cannot be "perfect" Christian, will always have a guilt complex, that he cannot please God.

One time the saint Abba Macarius was asked, "Can a person who is a sinner enter monasticism or not?" Abba Macarius answered, saying, "We have not come to monasticism because we are perfect, but because we want to be perfect. For if we said that only the perfect man may enter monasticism, there would be no one deserving of monasticism, for no one is perfect. Therefore, I press toward perfection, that I may forget those things which are behind and reach forward to those things which are ahead. Monasticism may be a path that helps [a person] in pressing on and reaching perfection." If Abba Macarius confessed his helplessness and imperfection, how do some of us think that they could be perfect and without sin on this earth?

Do the words of Paul the Apostle—"Therefore let us, as many as are mature[120], have this mind; and if in anything you think otherwise, God will reveal even this to you"[121]—mean that we consequently may live in sin? Undoubtedly not. They mean that, as long as we live on this earth, we have to know that we have in us the good and bad, and strengths and weaknesses, and we have to realize that the other person has in him the good and bad [too], and has strengths and weaknesses. And this [realization] would prevent me from labelling people, nor see myself as a good man or bad man. We are Christian, not because we are perfect, but because we press on, that we may be perfect, and we are in dire need for forgiveness and acceptance. Therefore, I need to be Christian, because, through Christianity, my sins are forgiven by the blood of the Lord Christ present on the altar, and I will be accepted in the mystery of the cross and the arms stretched on it.

My going to Church and my partaking of the Holy Mysteries everyday are an implicit confession that I am an imperfect person. And someone might say that he could not partake [of the Mysteries] because he is bad. But the truth is that I need to partake [of the Mysteries], because I too need

---

120 The word in the Arabic verse may be translated as "perfect."
121 Philippians 3:15.

forgiveness and acceptance.

It is necessary that we distinguish between the meaning of the ideal self accepting the true self, and of the ideal self condemning the true self.

By the word "condemnation" is meant an angry rejection or anger-filled guidance against the bad or against the true self because it has imperfections. What would the result be if the idea self treated the true self, with judgment, cruelty, condemnation, rejection, and anger? The true self would have a feeling of shame, guilt, and fear, and then, it would hide and deny itself. And a conflict would arise.

Paul the Apostle had discriminated between two kinds of sorrow, saying, "Now I rejoice, not that you were made sorry, but that your sorrow led to repentance. For you were made sorry in a godly manner, that you might suffer loss from us in nothing. For godly sorrow produces repentance leading to salvation, not to be regretted; but sorrow of the world produces death."[122] So, there is a sorrow according to God's will, and sorrow according to the world; one produces repentance leading to salvation, but sorrow according to the world produces death, which takes place when the ideal self judges the true self, rejects it and is angry with it. This [latter] kind of sorrow resembles Judas' sorrow. After he betrayed the Lord Christ, and sold Him for thirty pieces of silver, his ideal self began retaliating against him,

---

122   2 Corinthians 7:9–10.

saying, "How could you do this? How [could you] betray the Lord Christ and betray innocent blood?[123] You are utterly rejected, and there is no salvation to you. Your guilt is greater than what may be endured." And so, the ideal self continued severely judging the true self, condemning it, and pouring out woes upon him. Therefore, there was a conflict within him, resulting from a feeling of guilt, fear, and shame. And the result was that he went and hanged himself, because the ideal self sentenced the true self to death. And this is the sorrow that produces death.

As for acceptance, it is the ideal self's acceptance of the true self, because it knows its weaknesses and helplessness. By acceptance, here, we mean the acceptance of self, and not of sin in which this self [or soul] fell. And here, the ideal self is sorrowful, but this sorrow is a godly sorrow that produces repentance leading to salvation, not to be regretted. And this is exactly what happened with Peter who denied the Lord Christ. So the ideal self said to the true self, "Truly, Peter, you have sinned, but the Lord knows your weakness and He loves you. Do you know what He did with the woman caught in the very act? And do you remember when you asked Him, 'How often shall my brother sin against me, and I forgive him? Up to seven times?' and He answered you, 'I do not say to you, up to seven

---

123   See Matthew 27:4.

times, but up to seventy times seven.'[124] And because He knows that you are weak, He came to give you strength through the cross on which He was hanged, and to give you salvation and forgiveness."

Peter was truly sorrowful and wept, but he knew that he was accepted and loved, and that the Lord came for the sake of sinners and not for the sake of the righteous. This is the sorrow which is according to God's will, producing repentance leading to salvation, not to be regretted. And so, the relationship between the ideal self and true self becomes a relationship filled with love and acceptance, as was the Lord Christ's relationship with sinners. He accepted them, for He had promised that "the one who comes to Me I will by no means cast out."[125]

And so can the true self change and grow in repentance and in the path of perfection, forgetting those things which are behind and reaching forward to those things which are ahead, if we accepted the weak parts in us, and this will be a cause for healing, growth, and change.

The problem of many of the youth, and people in general, is that they hate themselves sometimes, and reproach it severely, and reject their true selves. This makes them fall into a greater sorrow, but even fall more [frequently] into sin, not knowing how to

---

124 Matthew 18:21–22.

125 John 6:37.

escape this [vicious] cycle.

But the person who accepts his true self, with its weakness, shortcomings, and helplessness, brings it to the light of Christ, as did the four friends who brought the paralytic to the Lord Christ, so He healed him.[126] The ideal self has to likewise bear the true self, bringing it to the Mystery of Confession before Christ, uncovering it, with all its weaknesses, so as to receive from Christ forgiveness, healing, and acceptance. There are many who run away from the Mystery of Confession, and even if they confess, they forcefully defend themselves, because the ideal self refuses to accept the true self with its weakness, forcing it to vanish [from sight] and not come to the light. So long as it has not been exposed to the light of Christ, and has not been revealed as it truly is, it will not be healed nor change.

This is the magnificence of our Christianity which has given us the Mystery of Confession, in which I reveal myself as it truly is, and declare to God my need for the touch of His hand and forgiveness from Him, saying to Him, "Say unto my soul, 'Your sins are forgiven.' And loose it from the its bonds and fetters." Therefore, the relationship between the ideal self and the true self has to be a relationship based on love. So the ideal self should not be ashamed of the true self. Likewise, the true self has to cling to the ideal self, as a target to press

---

126   See Mark 2:1–12.

on towards: "Be perfect."[127] And then it wants too to reach the image of God, and change from glory to glory,[128] "to be conformed to the image of His Son."[129]

Paul the Apostle presented to us a wonderful image of this conflict in the epistle to the Romans:

> For what I am doing, I do not understand. For what I will to do, that I do not practice; but what I hate, that I do. If, then, I do what I will not to do, I agree with the law that it is good. But now, it is no longer I who do it, but sin that dwells in me. For I know that in me (that is, in my flesh) nothing good dwells; for to will is present with me, but how to perform what is good I do not find. For the good that I will to do, I do not do; but the evil I will not to do, that I practice.[130]

Therefore, Christ came in order to settle this conflict. He brought about reconciliation. He has not only reconciled man with God or with his brother, but also reconciled man with himself. And this is very important. He has given him all the capabilities, so that his true self may grow to [the

---

127 Matthew 5:48.

128 See 2 Corinthians 3:18.

129 Romans 8:29.

130 Romans 7:15–19.

measure of] perfection through the ideal self.

In Ecclesiastes, he says:

> I have seen everything in my days of vanity: there is a just man who perishes in his righteousness, and there is a wicked man who prolongs life in his wickedness. Do not be overly righteous, nor be overly wise: why should you destroy yourself? Do not be overly wicked, nor be foolish: why should you die before your time? It is good that you grasp this, and also not remove your hand from the other; for he who fears God will escape them all.[131]

Here, by the statement "Do not be overly righteous," he means that you should accept yourself, with your weakness and helplessness, and do not let the ideal self reject the true self, appearing to be a righteous self[132] at all time, and do not use worldly, self-centered[133] wisdom, with which you deceive yourself and believe that you are overly righteous.

You have to know that you are called to perfection because you are a child of God, but have to know at the same time that you are human who has weaknesses and shortcomings, and there are things you are not able to do. Indeed, it is good that

---

131 Ecclesiastes 7:15–18.

132 Or: soul.

133 Or: sensual.

you hold on to your calling to perfection, and also it is good to not disregard your true self with what it has, for he who fears God benefits from all. There has to be a balance in the relationship between the ideal self and the true self, and balance means that a person knows that he has weaknesses, but at the same time he presses on toward perfection.

The Psalmist says, "Return, O LORD, deliver me! Oh, save me for Your mercies' sake! For in death there is no remembrance of You; in the grave who will give You thanks? I am weary with my groaning; all night I make my bed swim; I drench my couch with my tears. My eye wastes away because of grief; it grows old because of all my enemies."[134] Here the Psalmist states his goal, that is, to reach perfection, because if he died, he would not be able to do anything about pressing on towards perfection. Then he reveals the real self as it truly is: he weeps all night, and is sorrowful, because of his helplessness; therefore, he says, "Return, O LORD, deliver me! Oh, save me for Your mercies' sake!"

"For He knows our frame; He remembers that we are dust."[135] God knows our weakness, and that we are dust. So does He reject us because of that? No, for this [reason], he mentions, "As far as the east is from the west, so far has He removed our transgressions from us. As a father pities his

---

134 Psalm 6:4–7.
135 Psalm 103:14.

children, so the LORD pities those who fear Him."[136] And why does the Lord pity us? Because He knows our frame, that we are weak and sinful. The same thing is said by Paul the Apostle, "As it is written: 'There is none righteous, no, not one; there is none who understands; there is none who seeks after God.'"[137] Therefore, God gave us the Law, and the Lord Christ came and saved us, because we all need salvation from sin, and need the righteousness of Christ, too.

The ideal self in God's view and in my view

It is of importance that each of us ask themselves, "Is the image of the ideal self in my mind, the same as that which is in God's mind?" because sometimes the ideal self may be confused. Does perfection as I know it, have the same definition with God? For, often, what I imagine to be the ideal self differs from that which God created and which exists in His mind. I may characterize, for example, one of my needs as a bad thing, a weakness, or a disability, but God looks to it as a good thing, and that it is important for growth, healing, and building the self. Adam felt a need for another person to be with him, though he was present with God before the fall. And perhaps, some might interpret the need for another [person] as a bad thing, for it is better for the person

---

136 Psalm 103:12–13.
137 Romans 3:10–11.

to be strong and in no need of another at all. But God did not see that Adam's need as a bad thing, but good, and said, "It is not good that man should be alone."[138] For what is good is that Adam should have a helper comparable to him, and then God created Eve for him. Then the Scripture immediately after that says, "Then God saw everything that He had made, and indeed it was very good."[139] It is not only good, but very good. God has created us as people who grow through relationships.

There are some [people] who imagine that showing emotions is [considered] a weakness and a bad thing; therefore, he holds himself from crying, for if someone sees him crying, he will criticize him, because he is a man and is not supposed to cry, even though crying is one of the factors of the healing of the soul. If crying were a bad thing, how did the Lord Christ—glory be to Him—cry at Lazarus' tomb.

The image of the ideal self is usually formed in us through the upbringing method by which we were raised. So if I was taught from a young age that crying, or showing emotions and feelings, is a bad thing, I would grow up, and on my mind would be ingrained [the idea] that I have to suppress my feelings and not show them. And this is one of the complains we encounter in families, for the wife

---

138 Genesis 2:18.
139 Genesis 1:31.

may complain of her husband not expressing his feelings to her, even though he may be doing many good deeds.

Therefore, the definition of perfection in my mind has to be the same as the one in God's mind.

> *"These things keep young men from evil thoughts: reading the Holy Scriptures, setting aside laziness, rising up at night for prayer, being adorned with humility always."*
>
> —Abba Moses the Strong—

The struggle between the ideal self and the true self

The struggle between the ideal self and the true self may take one of four ways. It is also considered the struggle between good and evil. It is worthy of mentioning that three of them [i.e. these ways] do not achieve success, and this is what we will discuss in greater details.

The first way: Denying the bad (the true self)

If it happened that I was upset or angry with someone, I would try to suppress these feelings and overlook them, as though I were not angry with him. And there may be someone who causes harm, and then I have to set boundaries in my relationship with him, so that he does not continue in his abuse. But my ideal self sees that this matter is bad, for the loving, ideal person should not set boundaries to stop the abuse. The ideal self here denies [the existence of] what is bad and does not admit it, and it urges the true self not to feel angry or whatnot.

The dangerous thing is when the feelings of sin are aroused in a person, like lust, envy, or other feelings, so he tries to ignore their existence, and thinks that if these feelings were truly present, they would defile him. There is a difference, however, between a person who admits the existence of these feelings and then deals with them to make them godly feelings, and [a person who] ignores and suppresses them. When a person deals with these feelings and reveals them to the light of Christ, he is sanctified. But if he ignores and denies their existence, they will remain buried within him, and they may come out violently at some point in time, thereby causing devastation in his life.

This was what the scribes and Pharisees used to do. Therefore, the Lord said to them, "Woe to you, scribes and Pharisees, hypocrites! For you are like whitewashed tombs which indeed appear beautiful outwardly, but inside are full of dead men's bones and all uncleanness."[140]

Often there may be people in our lives, whom

---

140   Matthew 23:27.

we idolize and refuse [to believe] that there is in them any fault or anything bad. And if we happen to hear that one of these has sinned, we are shocked, especially if this person were one of the renowned leaders in the Church, and we forget then that all are but human, and that all have sinned and fall short of the glory of God[141]. For this reason we put an end to this struggle by denying the bad that is in us or in others.

Sometimes someone may feel that he has no mistakes, and if one of the priests invited this person to confess because he has not practiced this Mystery for a long time, he would answer saying that he does not have any mistakes to confess. A priest related that one day he went to visit a family, so he asked one of their sons about him not having confessed for many months. He answered, "I do not have sins to confess." Then the priest began asking him few questions, and this young man answered that he indeed had committed this and did that. So the priest said to him, "All these are sins." The young man looked to the priest and said, "I have come to you righteous, and left a sinner." The truth is that this young man was not lying when he said that he had not sinned, because he lived continually in a state of denial.

---

141 See Romans 3:23.

The second way: Denying the good (the ideal self)

What is meant by this is that, in the ideal self's dealing with the true self—or the struggle between good and evil [or bad]—we deny the existence of good completely, and we consider the relationship to be nothing but a charade, and nothing more than hypocrisy; for there is no one good ever. This may take place when a person is aware of his inability to achieve perfection, and his true self will never attain the ideal self. And he may reach a complete hardness of heart, and may live in sin, even [to the point] of denying God's existence in his life. Paul the Apostle expressed this matter when he described the state of people, saying:

> For the wrath of God is revealed from heaven against all ungodliness and unrighteousness of men, who suppress the truth in unrighteousness, because what may be known of God is manifest in them, for God has shown it to them. For since the creation of the world His invisible attributes [that is, the attributes we do not see with our eyes] are clearly seen, being understood by the things that are made, even His eternal power and Godhead, so that they are without excuse.[142]

---

142 Romans 1:18–20.

For we are able to see God's attributes, which we do not see with our eyes, through the creation. When I see the sun and stars and all the things that are made, I must confess that [there is] behind them a Creator. Paul the Apostle continues, saying:

> Because, although they knew God, they did not glorify Him as God, nor were thankful, but became futile in their thoughts, and their foolish hearts were darkened. Professing to be wise, they became fools, and changed the glory of the incorruptible God into an image made like corruptible man—and birds and four-footed animals and creeping things.[143]

They do not see within themselves any goodness, and since there is no goodness within them, they do not then see goodness outside [themselves]. Therefore, these people do not attempt to strive on the path of virtue. And they may not see any goodness in others, too, when they deal with them, always directing scathing criticism at them. For they see everything in them [i.e. others] as bad, and ask them to be perfectionists in everything.

There is a difference between the words perfect and perfectionist. Those who are perfectionists have what is called obsessive-compulsive [personality], who want everything to be perfect in an unrealistic way. Therefore, they may repeat a thing time

---

143 Romans 1:21–23.

and again, and it is an obsession. This obsessive-compulsive [personality] forces the person to repeat doing something tens of times, till it reaches perfection.

The third way: Attacking the bad

It means the struggle between good and bad [or evil], and attacking the bad and condemning it. This is the most common way to deal with the bad in us. For someone might say, for example, "I do not deserve anything because of the sin I am living in," and he judges and condemns himself severely and harshly. As we have previously said about Judas' ideal self reproving his real self, the matter is completely different from the reproof of the Holy Spirit in the dealings of the ideal self with the real self when it sins. This [latter] is like what happened with Peter the Apostle, for his sorrow was a sorrow producing repentance leading to salvation, not to be regretted.[144]

The fourth way: The ideal self's acceptance of the true self

This is the way we should adopt, and according to which we should act. It is the way of love and acceptance. In it, the ideal self accepts the true self, and [yet] admits its sins. But through repentance,

---

144 See 2 Corinthians 7:10.

confession and communion, it offers this self remission, and forgives it without harshness and condemnation from within. Sometimes we hear many people say the following statement: "I have confessed, and the priest read the absolution and said to me, 'That is it, God is not upset with you,' but I am not able to forgive myself." The statement, "I am not able to forgive myself," means that the ideal self is pressuring the true self, saying to it, "Even if God forgave you, I will not forgive you." And so, the person is tormented because he cannot forgive himself. He cannot actually accept the gift of remission and forgiveness from the hand of God, because the ideal self says to the true self that it is not worthy of forgiveness and remission. And the struggle continues, because the ideal self continually attacks the true self. But if it [i.e. the ideal self] accepts it with its weakness and helplessness, then remission is offered it from the hand of Christ, and through the Holy Mysteries, on the basis of them being a healing and growth for the soul[145], so the true self grows from glory to glory, till it becomes conformed to the image of His Son.

As the person has to train [himself] to accept the good and bad—here we are talking about accepting the bad, and not accepting sin—he may also accept the good and bad in others, knowing that others have weaknesses, and then he would not be disgusted by them. Our teacher Paul the Apostle

---

145 Or: self.

says, "And be kind to one another—[does 'to one another' mean the people who are good only? Of course not. Therefore, he also says]—tenderhearted, forgiving one another, even as God in Christ forgave you."[146] The statement "[this is] good and [that is] bad" will not be present in a person's vocabulary, because each of us has the good in him, and also the bad. Even the people, whom we see as extremely bad, are in their depths extremely good. Therefore, the good person who was in the depths of the right-hand thief, led him to repentance at the last moment of his life. Paul the Apostle says too:

> Therefore, as the elect of God, holy and beloved, put on tender mercies, kindness, humility, meekness, longsuffering; bearing with one another,—[undoubtedly, I would bear with something bad too]—and forgiving one another, if anyone has a complaint against another; even as Christ forgave you, so you also must do.[147]

And in the epistle to the Romans, he talks about love and acceptance, saying, "Therefore receive[148] one another, just as Christ also received us, to the glory of God."[149] And what about our own case

---

146 Ephesians 4:32.

147 Colossians 3:12–13.

148 The Arabic word used here in this verse may be translated into "accept."

149 Romans 15:7.

when Christ accepted us, and we were yet sinners!

It says in Proverbs, "He who covers a transgression seeks love, but he who repeats a matter separates friends."[150] If I learn that my brother has sinned, and I accept him and cover his sin, then I am seeking love, but if I begin speaking about his sin, and continue talking about him, I separate people.

"We should not snoop on people, and places, to discover others' sins. If the sins of others were presented to us, being forced upon us, we should not examine them nor turn to them."

—Abba Pimen the Solitary—

Since we are supposed to accept the good and bad, deal with both together, and confess their concurrent existence, then why does a person find it difficult to deal with the good and bad [together]? It is because God created man good, incorruptible, "then God saw everything that He had made, and indeed it was very good."[151] He did not create man, that he may deal with good and evil [or bad], but that he may deal with good only. God wanted to protect man from dealing with evil, so He gave him a commandment, that he [i.e. Adam] may stay away from this tree in order not to have knowledge of good and evil, because if he had this knowledge,

---

150 Proverbs 17:9.
151 Genesis 1:31.

he would begin dealing with evil, and would face a problem in this dealing, for he was created to deal with good only.

But man rejected God's protection, so he disobeyed Him and fell. Then he had to deal with good as well as evil, and as it is said in the Psalm, "And in sin my mother conceived me."[152] The person is born in sin, and therefore he has to deal with the good and evil.

In order for us to love and accept others, and forgive them, we must ourselves [first] have been filled with love, forgiveness, and acceptance, and have realized God's acceptance and forgiveness for us, and have felt His love. For we love because He first loved us.[153] The one who is filled with God's love and with the feeling that God has accepted him, is able to love, accept, and forgive. Therefore, Paul the Apostle says, "Receive[154] one another, just as Christ also received us, to the glory of God."[155]

We certainly feel Christ's acceptance of us in the Mysteries of the Church. The infant is born in sin, and though he does not understand yet, his parents bring him to the priest to baptize him. And he comes out of Baptism wearing white clothes, which means that he has become righteous and has been

---

152 Psalm 51:5.

153 See 1 John 4:19.

154 The Arabic word used here in this verse may be translated into "accept."

155 Romans 15:7.

purified of sin and the old man, through the water of Baptism. So the Baptism and righteousness which he took, did he receive them by grace, or because he was worthy of them? He did nothing deserving of this grace. Therefore, Baptism gives the person a very profound feeling of God's acceptance, love, and forgiveness. And after Baptism, he is anointed with the Mystery of Myron, through which the Holy Spirit dwells in us: "Do you not know that you are the temple of God and that the Spirit of God dwells in you?"[156] So did the infant do anything to deserve that God dwells in him? And likewise, the Mysteries are a grace invisible. And on the same day of his baptism and anointing with Myron, the infant partakes of the Body of Christ, that is, he unites with Christ, and he abides in Christ and Christ abides in him, so he receives eternal life: "Whoever eats My flesh and drinks My blood has eternal life."[157] He did not receive eternal life based on his worthiness; it is grace from God. And this makes the infant, while still young, realize that he is loved and accepted, and that God forgives him, a matter that makes him able to love, accept, and forgive, as God accepted him. Therefore, depriving infants of the Mysteries, means in reality depriving them of love, forgiveness, and acceptance, because when we say to the infant that he is still young and will not understand, this consequently means that he does

---

156 1 Corinthians 3:16.

157 John 6:54.

not deserve to be loved, and for his sin, which he was born in, to be forgiven, and for the Holy Spirit to dwell in him. And then he cannot deal [properly] with the evil which exists in the world.

One of the most wonderful stories elucidating the topic of [how to] deal with what is bad, is the story of the sinful woman in Simon's house. She went into the house, and Simon the Pharisee was of the type [of people] who attacks what is bad and judges it. Nevertheless, Simon denies the bad that is in himself, for he sees himself righteous. He resembles the Pharisee who prayed, saying, "God, I thank You that I am not like other men—extortioners, unjust, adulterers, or even as this tax collector. I fast twice a week; I give tithes of all that I possess."[158] Simon would deny the bad concerning himself, and [yet] would see and judge it concerning others, even to the point that he saw in the Lord Christ—glory be to Him—something bad, and judged Him, saying, "This Man, if He were a prophet, would know who and what manner of woman this is who is touching Him, for she is a sinner."[159] The Lord Christ, however, did not deny the bad that was in the woman, but saw the good that was in her, because she loved much. He knew that she was a sinful woman because He said, "Her sins, which are many, are forgiven, for she loved much. But to whom little is forgiven, the same loves

158 Luke 18:11–12.
159 Luke 7:39.

little."[160] Therefore, He said to the woman, "Your sins are forgiven," confirming that there is in her [something] bad, yet He did not attack her, because He looked to the good that was in her and accepted her with love, forgave her and defended her. This matter is what converted the sinful woman into a saint.

Attacking what is bad, and judging it, destroys the person. But accepting the sinner, and offering him love and forgiveness, makes him change and transform from image to image, and from glory to glory to be conformed to the image of His Son.[161] The one who could deal [well] with what is bad is the spiritually mature person. In the story of the sinful woman, Simon was not successful spiritually, despite his good knowledge of the law and commandments. The Person of the Lord Jesus Christ, however, is the source of all maturity and knowledge. He dealt with the woman, as He also dealt with what is bad in Simon; therefore, He accepted him and began teaching him, giving him a parable: "There was a certain creditor who had two debtors. One owed five hundred denarii, and the other fifty."[162] The Lord Christ neither attacked nor judged anyone.

And when Christ poured the woes upon the scribes and Pharisees in the twenty-third chapter of the Gospel according to St. Matthew, He did

---

160 Luke 7:47.

161 See Romans 8:29.

162 Luke 7:41.

not attack individuals, but groups of people. And in the case of some of the individuals with whom Christ dealt with severity, [He showed us that] there is a way to deal with the bad, with what we may call "tough love." It is love, which may appear to harbor harshness, but its goal is to lead the person to repentance, as Paul the Apostle did with the sinner in the Church in Corinth. He judged that this person should be put away, but after he was put away, he wept and searched for him, and he sent Titus to ask about him, until he was reassured regarding him, then he asked the Church to assure him of the love. This is a kind of love, and is being firm in dealing with gross mistakes. Paul the Apostle offered grace and truth.

We should not always say about somebody that he is evil, and that we are not able to deal with him. But if we looked at him as a person who has [both] the good and bad, then we are able to deal with him.

Theories on the growth of the human being affirm that a child, when [he is] born, realizes from the first moment what is good and bad; everything to him is either white or black, either good or bad. He separates everything in the world, people and even himself, into good and bad. The infant cries when he wants to eat, and if they are delayed on him for three or four minutes, he begins screaming with a louder voice, because he feels that they have neglected him and have treated him badly. But when his own food is given him, he calms down, because he feels that the people around him are good. The mother, for him, is either bad or good, for there is no difference between them. But when he grows up and becomes older, he begins to realize that there is nothing that is good on its own, nor bad on its own, but the two things exist together. If the child, during his childhood, receives a sufficient amount of love, acceptance, and forgiveness, this will help him, when he grows up, to deal well with the bad. And vice versa, if he does not experience compassion and love, he will see others as bad, and that the world is entirely bad, having nothing good. An inward hatred will grow within him against the world, his family and those around him.

Therefore, it is important to be cautious of the danger that a mother leaves her child to a nanny, to take care of raising him, because a nanny cares only about his food and changing his clothes, but she will not offer him [sufficient] love. And when the mother comes back from work, at the end of the day, she may be exhausted and incapable of offering him the love the child needs.

On the contrary, there are fathers and mothers who love their children excessively, spoil them, and consent to all their requests, and even if the child makes a mistake, they do not chasten nor discipline him. Therefore, "the world" to them is all good, but when they go out to the real world, and someone gives them a criticism, a harmless comment, or an observation, they are greatly troubled, becoming hypersensitive, because they have not learned how to forgive anybody if he sins against them

God, in His dealings with us, does not mark our sins nor keep a record of them, but He works[163] with our weakness, reproves us of sin, and leads us to repentance. In the Psalm that begins by saying, "Out of the depths I have cried to You, O LORD," it says, "If You, LORD, should mark iniquities, O Lord, who could stand? But there is forgiveness with You."[164] There is a difference between the parents who mark the iniquities and weaknesses of their children, repeating it to them, and the parents who accept the weakness, work with them [i.e. their children], and lead them to repentance. God deals with us with kindness; therefore, the Scripture says, "Not knowing that the goodness of God leads you to repentance?"[165]

We all have to realize, as fathers and mothers, as servants and clergy, that the time wherein we exist is a time for reformation, a time for redemption and visitation, a time for reforming what is bad, and accepting the truth of ourselves, that we are weak, and we will reform this bad [aspect]. This is not the time for condemnation and punishment, because "He has appointed a Day for recompense, on which He will appear to judge the world in righteousness,

---

163 Literally: deals.

164 Psalm 130:3–4.

165 Romans 2:4.

and give each one according to his deeds."[166] It is the time for repentance and salvation, and not for destruction and demolition. Therefore, whenever a child grows up in an atmosphere of love and acceptance, he learns to be sorrowful over failure, what is bad, and weakness, without [falling into] despair and defeat. We refrain from committing sin, because we love God, others, and ourselves. The ten commandments are divided into two groups: the first group, consisting of the first four commandments, regulates God's relationship with man. The remaining six commandments regulate a man's relationship with his brother. They used to summarize these ten commandments into two commandments. The first four commandments were summarized into, "Love the Lord your God." The last six commandments were summarized into, "Love your neighbor as yourself." The Lord gave us the commandment, which is love, and not merely "right and wrong."

As an example, if there were a person you do not know and have no loving relationship with him, then [if] you sinned against him and cursed him, the thing that would trouble you the most is that you have done something wrong, and perhaps you do not care about fixing the mistake, because you do not care about this person at all, and so he has gone his way. But if you sinned against someone you love, your focus is not that you did something

---

166 The Divine Liturgy According to St. Basil – Agios (Holy).

wrong, but that you hurt this person, and you care about restoring the relationship with him and about getting reconciled with him, that the loving relationship may return. Likewise, sin is a wound to the loving relationship with God. Therefore, your focus is that you have hurt God, and that you are reconciled with Him, which makes it easy for you to repent. We pray in the Prayer of the Fraction, "So be sorrowful, O my soul, for your sins that caused these sufferings to Your compassionate Redeemer. Portray His wound before you, and hope in Him when the enemy rages against you."[167]

And as the person matures spiritually, he views his relationship with God and with others as a loving relationship; therefore, I am a loved person in God's eyes, for the Lord died on my behalf upon the cross. And when I realize that I am loved, I am able to love myself, pardon and forgive it, and accept forgiveness from God, then I live in the joy of repentance. Paul the Apostle confirms this meaning, by saying:

> For by one offering He has perfected forever those who are being sanctified. But the Holy Spirit also witnesses to us; for after He had said before, "This is the covenant that I will make with them after those days, says the Lord: I will put My laws into their hearts, and in their minds I will write them," then He adds, "Their sins and their lawless deeds

---

167 The Divine Liturgy – Fraction to the Son: O Only-begotten Son.

I will remember no more."[168]

God cares that our relationship with Him be a loving relationship. Therefore, He has given us the Mysteries, to say to us, "Every time you commit a sin, come and confess it, offer repentance for it, and wash it away through Communion." Repentance in this case is reconciliation to God, as Paul the Apostle says, "Now then, we are ambassadors for Christ, as though God were pleading through us: we implore you on Christ's behalf, be reconciled to God."[169]

There is a difference between the life of virtue that is based on love, and the life of virtue that is based on fear; that is, I want to do good so that I will not be cast into hell, and because I am afraid of God's anger.

Accordingly, if the ideal self forgave with love the true self all its mistakes, and accepted it, then this love will grow in the true self, so it will mature and change from glory to glory,[170] to become conformed to the image of His Son.[171]

---

168 Hebrews 10:14–17.
169 2 Corinthians 5:20.
170 See 2 Corinthians 3:18.
171 See Romans 8:29.

Questions and Answers

I would like to share with you, dear reader, some of the questions frequently posed to me. Perhaps you may find some answers to questions you have.

How should I deal with my partner who has no feelings at all, who never listens, and who does not confess his feelings?

It is said that a man's confession of his weaknesses constitutes 80% of the change. So if the partner realizes that not expressing one's feelings is not God's will, and that it is a weakness in them, then this [in itself] is a substantial thing. The reason for this may be that the person was raised and grew up in a home where he learned that expressing one's feelings is a kind of weakness, leading people to exploiting him; therefore, he resorts to protecting himself by hiding behind a very high wall. It may be that he expressed himself at some point in his life, but was hurt, and then he does not want to be hurt again. What we need [on our part] is to surround this person with an atmosphere of love. This love resembles drops of water falling on a rock, drop by drop, until this rock crumbles.

If such a person becomes exposed to an atmosphere of love, grace, acceptance, and tolerance, which may be challenging on the wife's part, then he will change. But when the wife does not come across feelings of love, she may say, "Until when do I continue giving him my love?" The matter, however, requires that we do not take things personally, and that we understand that his lack of expression of his feelings has something to do with his upbringing and his way of thinking about his ideal self. This understanding liberates the wife from the bonds that he does not love her, and she begins to say, "He loves me but he does not know how to express his feelings. Therefore, I will teach him how to do so, by expressing my feelings and offering him love." My advice to you is that you should not look at this matter personally, because you will not be able to offer [him] love, except if you look at this as a matter related to his personality, education, and upbringing, and that God has put you in his way, to offer him the love that would heal him, change him, and make him [himself] able to offer love in a safe environment. Undoubtedly, you will not be able to do this with your power; therefore, you need prayer, support from the Holy Spirit, and the work of grace in your life.

I want to be spiritually mature, but I can never be so. I want to love God, and do all that He loves, and be in a relationship with Him, but my life is filled with anxiety and fear of everything?

I would say to you that you should approach God with your true self, and enter into a relationship with Him as you would establish a relationship with any person. Start by talking with Him, get to know Him, and spend time with Him. If you felt fear, say to Him, "Lord, I have fear," and He will interact with you. Nathanael had doubts but he did not put on the appearance of righteousness, so when Philip said to him, "We have found the Messiah... who is of Nazareth." Nathanael did not resort to what the prophecies said, but expressed his doubts, saying, "Can anything good come out of Nazareth?"[172]

Come with your weakness, helplessness, and the doubt that is you, and be in touch with Christ. When Nathanael came to the Lord Christ with his real self, the Lord treated the doubt that was in him, even until he said at the end, "Rabbi, You are the Son of God! You are the King of Israel!"[173] And this is also what happened with the Samaritan woman. She said to the Lord Christ, "I see that You are a Jew,"[174] that is, You are an enemy. But with the development[175] that happened in her, she said to Him, "Are You

---

172 John 1:46.

173 John 1:49.

174 See John 4:9.

175 Literally: maturation.

greater than our father Jacob?"[176] After that she said to Him, "Sir, I perceive that You are a prophet."[177] Then she added after that, "I know that Messiah is coming (who is called Christ). When He comes, He will tell us all things."[178] Then she came out to the light and preached saying, "Come, see a Man who told me all things that I ever did. Could this be the Christ?"[179]

Enter into a relationship with God, pray, read the Holy Scriptures, persevere in attending Church, confess and reveal your real self, with which enter into a relationship with God. Present your fear and your anxiety, in a realistic way, before God, and God will heal your soul.

I do confess, but have not benefited from my confession, because I have not been given any rule or [spiritual] exercise?

Believe me that the matter does not need rules and exercises. What does it mean if the priest says [to you], pray, read the Holy Scriptures, fast, and go to Church! Do you not know all these practices! Your presence in the Mystery of Confession is the revealing of yourself in the light of Christ, which would help you change. Let not your view of sin

---

176   John 4:12.

177   John 4:19.

178   John 4:25.

179   John 4:29.

merely be "right" and "wrong;" rather let your view of it be that this loving relationship is harmed because of sin, and consequently, how are you reconciled to God?

Next time, confess without thinking about sin as being right and wrong, but you desire to reconcile to God who loved you fervently, whom you love fervently too.

My father and mother hunt for anything bad that I may have done. And if I do something good, they thank me right there and then, and the matter is over, but always remember the bad things. What advice do you give them?

I would like to give you an advice yourself. Keep in mind that they do thank you for the good things you have done. It is possible that the bad things continually recur; therefore, every time you do it again, they remember too what you have previously done.

I also would like to advise the parents to always encourage their children. The Holy Scripture says, "Comfort[180] the fainthearted, uphold the weak, be patient with all."[181] And whenever you encourage your children, are long-suffering toward them, and support them, this makes them change to the better.

---

180 This word in Arabic may be translated into "encourage." But it appears as "comfort" in NKJV.
181 1 Thessalonians 5:14.

Constant and searing criticism, and not giving them any words of encouragement, will not help them change, and perhaps contrarily, even if the child did something good, he would do it out of fear, and not out of love.

My son is very stubborn, especially that his father spoils him, because he does not see him often—what do I do?

This *is* a problem, actually. The father may be the one scolding the child, while the mother is the one spoiling and indulging him, and the opposite may happen too. And so, the child takes advantage of this discrepancy in treatment between the father and mother. Therefore, there has to be balance between the father's indulgence and the mother's firmness. I advise that the father should be firmer in his dealings with the son, and that the mother should offer the son greater love. Consequently, the stubbornness will disappear, and there will be a greater balance between firmness and love.

This question is considered the focal point of my life, and is the reason of its destruction. I run away from my real personality through daydreaming, and I become engrossed in it until I reach the ideal personality. So what is the solution, to stop getting engrossed in this, which has nearly brought my life to ruin?

I would like to congratulate you first for being able to discover your weakness, and for realizing that you run away in your imagination from the real personality to the ideal personality. This realization is 80% of the change. So you have to ask for help from God, to help you enter into a true relationship with Him.

Stand before God, and before your father of confession, and reveal your true self with all its weaknesses, without making it appear beautiful, without adding your final touches, and without seeking excuses for yourself. I want you to enter into a relationship with God, through your true self, and say to Him, "Lord, here is my soul. Please, heal it."

When daydreaming wars against you, take a brave decision, sign your mind with the sign of the cross, ask the Holy Spirit for help, and cease from these dreams immediately and courageously. Then occupy yourself with something edifying. If you serve in visitation, decide to go out for visitation. And gradually you will find yourself to have begun to love your true self which you used to run away from; to have accepted and loved this true self, because God loves it; to have accepted it too, because God has accepted it; and to have forgiven it, because God has truly forgiven it.

God desires to take your true self and heal it. But you hide it from Him. He stands at the door of your true self, asking you to open to Him. You erect a barrier, through your ideal self, between God and your true self. Open the door once more, love yourself, reveal it to the light of Christ, and He will take your self, in truth, and will do to it what Paul the Apostle said, "That He might sanctify and cleanse her with the washing of water by the word, that He might present her to Himself a glorious church, not having spot or wrinkle or any such thing."[182]

And glory be to our God forever. Amen.

✠ ✠ ✠

---

182 Ephesians 5:26–27.